**LIVING IN MONNIKENHEIDE
CARE, INCLUSION AND ARCHITECTURE**

Gideon Boie (editor)

Gideon Boie, Sofie De Caigny, Fredie Floré, Vjera Sleutel,
Thomas Vanderveken, Heleen Verheyden and Erik Wieërs

Kurt Deruyter (photography)

Flanders Architecture Institute

CONTENTS

- 5   Foreword
  Sofie De Caigny
- 7   Introduction: A Testing Ground for Care Architecture
  Gideon Boie
- 15   Living with a Disability: A Typological Overview
  Gideon Boie
- 33   At Home in the Care Centre: A Look Inside
  Fredie Floré
- 49   Architecture of Presence
  Heleen Verheyden
- 57   Caring for the Landscape of Care
  Gideon Boie and Vjera Sleutel

- 73   Dwellings at Monnikenheide
  Gideon Boie and Vjera Sleutel
  - 73   Demeester residence, *Luc Van den Broeck* (1970)
    Short-Stay home, *Bruno Boulanger* (1973)
    Staff building, *Bruno Boulanger* (1973)
    Monnikenbos, *Luc Van den Broeck* (1980)
    Monnikenhuis, *Luc Van den Broeck* (1980)
    Werkhuis, *Mark Depreeuw* (1985)
  - 80   Seppenshuis, *bOb Van Reeth/ArchitectenWerkGroep* (1997)
  - 86   Annexe to Demeester residence, *Maarten Van Severen* (2000)
  - 90   Huis aan de Voorne, *Huiswerk architecten* (2003)
  - 96   Main building, Therapy Pool and Laundry, *Architectuurgroep Jo Peeters* (2003)
  - 100   Huis aan de Kerk, *Vermeiren De Coster Architecten* (2004)
  - 106   Open kamer, *Richard Venlet* (2006)
  - 108   Zonnebloem, *Architectuurgroep Jo Peeters* (2010)
  - 112   Huis aan 't Laar, *51N4E* (2013)
  - 118   De Eiken, *UR architects* (2016)
  - 124   Monnikenbos, *UR architects* (2020)
  - 130   Villa Kameleon, *FELT architecture & design* (2021)

- 145   Architecture That Makes People More Beautiful
  Sofie De Caigny
- 153   Vivre, C'est Faire Vivre
  Thomas Vanderveken
- 159   Afterword: On and Off Monnikenheide
  Erik Wieërs

- 160   Biographies
- 160   Colophon

Speech by Wivina Demeester at the laying of the foundation stone of Monnikenbos on 5 May 1979. In the background stands Gilbert (Bert) Hertecant, then chairman of the board © Monnikenheide Archives

FOREWORD

For the past fifty years, a special community has had its home among the majestic spruces and oaks of the forest of Zoersel. Some 200 people with mental and physical disabilities live there together in collective homes. The story of Monnikenheide began in 1973, when Wivina and Paul Demeester, with the help of supporters, opened the first 'short-stay home' on a plot donated by Paul's father, Jozef Demeester. The name refers to the Cistercian monks (Monniken-) who in the eighteenth century farmed the then heathland (-heide). Since it was founded, Monnikenheide has continued to evolve, both on its own land and in the adjacent subdivision and village of Zoersel.

To my mind, Monnikenheide is a radical experiment: radical in its rejection of the old logic of separation and invisibility, experimental in the principle underlying its architecture, one that embraces the otherness of every fellow human being. Monnikenheide is one of the few care institutions to give shape to authentic intersubjectivity, as advocated by philosopher Simone de Beauvoir. Equivalence comes from recognizing the other in his or her individuality. The collective homes give material expression to this insight. The result is a unique architecture at the intersection of privacy and connection, support and independence, otherness and what is understood as normality.

Each design question is approached with an open outlook and gives rise to an architectural experiment that responds to the evolving needs of residents and insights of carers. Young designers are often given plenty of opportunities in this respect. The oldest buildings are carefully adapted to meet developing insights – this too is unique in a sector where building something new is a matter of course. Over a span of fifty years, a rich catalogue of design knowledge has thus been created, as this book demonstrates.

A second feminist adage resonates at Monnikenheide: the personal is political. The small and the large do not exist without each other. The change in care that Paul and Wivina Demeester pursued for their own child is something they put into practice with Monnikenheide. In her role as minister in several governments, Wivina Demeester used the knowledge and expertise gained in the process. Both care policy and architecture culture in this country are indebted to her direct experiences in Zoersel. At Monnikenheide, care interconnects with architecture, politics and our general view of humanity and society.

We embraced Gideon Boie's proposal to tell the architectural history of this remarkable place in a book for the first time. After all, the Flanders Architecture Institute is convinced that Monnikenheide is an international reference in the field of care architecture. The architectural essays in this book place Monnikenheide in a broader evolution of care and architecture and reveal the unique expertise that has accumulated there over the past fifty years. The Flanders Architecture Institute hopes that Monnikenheide can inspire the care architecture of the future.

Sofie De Caigny
Director Flanders Architecture Institute

INTRODUCTION
A TESTING GROUND FOR CARE ARCHITECTURE
Gideon Boie

The history of Monnikenheide begins in 1967 with the birth of Steven, the firstborn son of Wivina and Paul Demeester-De Meyer.[1] The young couple was told by the doctor that it would be impossible to raise the boy with Down syndrome at home. At the time, it was quite common to house children with mental disabilities in the margins of psychiatric institutions. Discovering the world of persons with disabilities strengthened the conviction of the young couple that things could be done differently. A visit to Stropstraat in Ghent, the main campus of the Brothers of Charity, marked a breaking point.[2] The historic site symbolized institutional care in asylums for people with all kinds of illnesses and infirmities.

The desire grew to work, not only on adapted housing for their own family, but also on alternative accommodation for persons with mental disabilities.[3] An internship at Maria Roepaan in the Netherlands and contact with the practice of Bengt Nirje and Niels Erik Bank-Mikkelsen in Denmark provided inspiration about the inclusion of persons with mental disabilities. Inclusion also means the normalization of living and housing conditions in the form of family-sized supported-living housing. The approach put forward by Cornelis B. Bakker and Marianne K. Bakker-Rabdau strengthened the belief in the right to specific territorial needs and desires, also for persons with mental disabilities.[4] Inspiration later also came from a visit to L'Arche, an initiative for integrated housing communities set up by Jean Vanier in Compiègne.[5]

Participation in a three-day course run by the Lodewijk de Raet Foundation in 1968 introduced Wivina and Paul Demeester to architecture. The course aimed to inspire people who were going to build. The agenda included a visit to architect Renaat Braem's house in Antwerp. The initiation course marked the beginning of years of striving for good architecture, both in the couple's private home and in the development of Monnikenheide. During the course, Wivina and Paul met like-minded people with whom they founded the non-profit organization Monnikenheide in 1969. The non-profit wanted to build a 'short-stay home', as they called it, for children with mental disabilities in order to temporarily relieve parents – at the time, a one-of-a-kind initiative.

The search for a suitable building site led the couple to visit Paul's parents to talk about a piece of land in the vast Zoerselbos nature reserve – the deed of donation refers to 'De Schaapskooi' – which the family owned. In the first half of the twentieth century, the domain was owned by baron van de

1. Cover Dutch edition of *No Trespassing!* (*Verboden toegang*, 1976) from the library of the Demeester family.

Put and from 1952 by the non-profit organization Medische Inrichting en Openluchtwerken Sint-Godelieve (Medical Institution and Open-Air Works Saint Godelieve), an initiative by Fr. Frans-Bertrand Janssens OP who organized vacations for children there. After the initiative went out of business, part of the land was sold in 1957 to Jozef Demeester, director of the non-profit. On 24 June 1970, Jozef Demeester and Rachel Jacobs, Paul's parents, donated a plot of woodland to the non-profit organization Monnikenheide and a second plot to the couple. This allowed the non-profit to start work on the realization of its dream.

The name chosen was inspired by the indication on the Ferraris map where *'Monincken Heijde'* refers to the reclamation of the land by Cistercian monks. The exceptional location in the Kempen woods marked a giant leap from the ancient mental asylum to the Flemish housing idyll. Over the years, a string of residential facilities for people with mental disabilities would be built there, on the fault line between a nature reserve and an ever-expanding suburban subdivision, a typical settlement pattern in Flanders. The houses, scattered across the estate, are intended to house eight residents who live together in a family-sized supported-living context. The surrounding streets were used strategically to give the various houses their own addresses. Later, there would also be houses at strategic locations in the village and subdivision.

To develop Monnikenheide, Wivina and Paul Demeester systematically called on reputed architects and young, promising designers. The architects for the conversion of the short-stay home into the main building and the conversion of the villa were approached on the advice of bOb Van Reeth, the designer of Seppenshuis who in 1998 was appointed as the first Flemish Government Architect. For Huis aan de Voorne and Huis aan de Kerk, newly graduated architects active within the *Meesterproef* of the Flemish Government Architect were given a chance. The later design assignments for Huis aan 't Laar and De Eiken/Monnikenbos were awarded after a limited selection process inspired by the Open Call of the Flemish Government Architect.

The involvement of so many different architects ensured a variation on the same theme of the normalization of housing for people with mental disabilities. Each successive building project bolstered normalization: learning from experience, responding to the special needs of residents and looking for new possibilities. From the start, Monnikenheide also aspired to be a knowledge centre focused on exchange, symbolized in Seppenshuis. However, the combined architecture at Monnikenheide also embodies a special design intelligence, created out of everyday conversation and experimentation in the care centre, not through set theories, typologies and forms.[6]

Engagement with the functioning of architecture culture in Flanders is a constant in Monnikenheide's history. A member of the Flemish Christian Democrat Party (CD&V), Wivina Demeester served as minister and state secretary in several federal and regional governments between 1985 and 1999, with various competences in, among others, finance, budget, healthcare, welfare and public administration. In this capacity, she played a decisive role in the development of architecture culture in Flanders. She created

2. Preliminary design of the short-stay home by architect Juan Meyers, 1969. © Monnikenheide Archives and Juan Meyers

Medisch Sekretariaat van Sint-Jozefkliniek - Bethaniënhuis
vzw Gezondheidszorg CoVaBe

Handelslei 123
2160 ST.-ANTONIUS-ZOERSEL
Tel. (031) 83.22.31 - 83.22.41

Onze ref. :
Uw ref. :

Aan Mevrouw PLESSERS,
Directrice van Monnikenbos
Kasteeldreef 3
2153   ZOERSEL

St.Antonius-Zoersel, 7.2.1980.

Zeer geachte Mevrouw,

Wij vernemen dat weldra het home voor mentaal gehandicapten Monnikenbos onder Uw leiding zijn deuren zal openstellen. Twee onzer patiënten zullen kunnen overgeplaatst worden vanuit het psychiatrisch ziekenhuis naar Uw home, op aanvraag der ouders; hiervoor dank ik U ten zeerste.

In ons ziekenhuis verblijven nog meerdere mentaal gehandicapten, die -volgens de huidige strekkingen, die U wel kent- zouden moeten overgeplaatst worden naar home's, die een begeleiding en behandeling kunnen geven, die meer aan hun mentale handicap aangepast is.

Zoudt U bereid zijn nog meerdere dezer patiënten over te nemen ? Zo ja, zou U dan ons Uw opnamecriteria willen mededelen, zodat we U enkele kandidaturen kunnen voorstellen.

Van deze gelegenheid wil ik ook gebruik maken om U te verzekeren dat wij steeds tot iedere samenwerking bereid zijn; zou bv. één Uwer pupillen tijdelijk psychisch of psychotisch decompenseren, dan zijn wij steeds bereid haar (want wij nemen enkel vrouwen op) tijdelijk in onze psychiatrische afdeling te behandelen.

Indien U zoudt wensen over dit alles eens mondeling wat uitvoeriger te praten, bent U steeds welkom in het Psychiatrisch Centrum Bethaniënhuis; zoudt U wel zo vriendelijk willen zijn mij tevoren telefonisch van Uw komst te verwittigen.

Met oprechte hoogachting,

Dr.A.NUYTS,
Hoofdgeneesheer.

Letter from Dr. A. Nuyts (chief psychiatrist at Sint Jozefskliniek – Bethaniënhuis in Zoersel) to Mrs. Gilberte (Gib) Plessers (director of Monnikenbos) requesting the transfer of two patients from the psychiatric hospital to Monnikenheide suggesting that 'according to current trends, which you are well aware of', people with a mental disability should be transferred to homes (7 February, 1980). © Monnikenheide Archives

Dhr. A. NUYTS
Hoofdgeneesheer Bethaniëhuis
Handelslei 123
2160   St. Anthonius - Zoersel

Zoersel, 15 februari 1980
GP/hv/775/80

Geachte Heer,

Wij hebben met belangstelling uw brief gelezen en wij verheugen ons om uw steun en medewerking.

Zoals U bekend is zal 'Monnikenbos' het nieuwe bezigheidshome, werken met 20 niet werkende-mentaal gehandicapte mannen en vrouwen, vanaf 21 jaar.
Wij kunnen zeker de strekking waarin gepoogd wordt mentaal gehandicapten uit de psychiatrie over te plaatsen maar U begrijpt dat een opname-capaciteit van 20? dit 'grote' probleem niet zal oplossen.
Wel zullen wij kunnen helpen, zoals dit nu ook reeds het geval is, voor twee- of drie gasten die bij U verblijven.

De opname-criteria zijn dus :
- mentaal gehandicapt - niet werkend in beschutte werkplaats.
- 21 jaar en ouder
- zwaar verzorgende gasten met permanent medisch toezicht worden niet opgenomen.
- andere bijkomende handicaps vormen geen probleem.
- wij houden rekening bij de samenstelling van de leefgroepen met verhouding - geslacht
  - leeftijd
  - aktief niveau
  - bijkomende handicaps.

Zoals U voorstelt kunnen wij hierover nog een uitgebraider gesprek voeren, waarvoor ik U in de komende dagen zal kontakteren.

Met bijzondere hoogachting

Positive answer from Mrs. Gib Plessers to Dr. A Nuyts with the list of admission criteria after first suggesting the few new homes will never fully solve the issue of people with a mental disability staying in psychiatry (15 February, 1980). © Monnikenheide Archives

the position of Flemish Government Architect and was chairman of the board of directors of the Flanders Architecture Institute from 2004 to 2022.[7]

Monnikenheide can be seen as a culmination of interests in care, architecture and politics. Or, alternatively, we could say that the Demeester couple's search for an adapted housing solution for persons with disabilities sowed the seeds of years of engagement in care, architecture and politics in Flanders. Whatever the case, Monnikenheide presents itself, fifty years after its foundation, as a testing ground for care architecture – although the modifier 'care' should not detract from the ambition to build normal homes that you and I would want to live in just as much. 'Architecture makes people more beautiful' is a one-liner that, for Wivina Demeester, does not just apply to people with mental disabilities. At best, the care programme adds a dash of beauty to our way of living together in village and city.

The architectural production at Monnikenheide can be divided roughly into three periods. The initial period from 1970 to 1985 comprises the first settlement, with the house for the Demeester family, the Short-Stay Home, the Staff Building, the Permanent Residence and the Werkhuis. The construction of Seppenshuis can be seen as the conclusion of this period. In the second period, from 2000 onwards, sites outside the estate were sought, both in the ribbon development (Huis aan de Voorne) and on the village square (Huis aan de Kerk). In parallel, the first buildings were renovated and extended, a contrast with the trend for permanent new construction in the care sector. 'You don't demolish your own home just like that, do you?!', Wivina Demeester retorted, many years later. The third construction period began after 2010, with new buildings (Huis aan 't Laar en De Eiken) and renovations (Monnikenbos) at strategic locations on the estate and just around the corner in the subdivision (Villa Kameleon).

A new development occurred at Monnikenheide with the acquisition of Huis aan den Donk (2013) in Zandhoven, a joint venture with care home Hooidonk of the Christian Mutual Insurance Fund, and De Bast (2015) in Oostmalle, part of the public-private centre development De Notelaar. During that same period, the life's work of Wivina and Paul Demeester in 2015 came under the aegis of the non-profit association Emmaüs, a grouping of twenty-four care facilities active in the province of Antwerp under the direction of Inge Vervotte, party colleague and former Flemish minister of welfare. The merger of Monnikenheide with the non-profit Spectrum in 2020 was carried out in order to scale things up under the Emmaüs umbrella and to strengthen operations with branches such as De Dijk in Gooreind and Het Loo in Westmalle. The presence in the village centre was strengthened by the purchase in 2022 of party hall Smoutmolen near the church to provide day care for people with disabilities.[8]

3. Wivina Demeester with the scale model of the short-stay home, image accompanying the article on Monnikenheide in *De Standaard* (21 April 1971).

This publication chronicles the history of Monnikenheide from an architectural perspective for the first time. Several projects from Monnikenheide quickly gained iconic status in Flemish architecture culture. They have been frequently published, but never documented and commented on together. Less iconic projects are no less fascinating when it comes to inclusion and normalization. Moreover, you cannot consider one residence in Monnikenheide in isolation from the others, as designs usually interact and build on each other. A residential care centre is not something you build in one day. Because the branches have a different genesis, they are not included in the overview.

The case studies offer a chronological overview of architectural production at Monnikenheide since the early years, in both words and images. Compiled by Vjera Sleutel and myself, the case studies came about on the basis of interviews with the architects, clients and staff involved. In each case, we describe how architecture is embedded in a special care vision that adapts flexibly according to needs and possibilities and the zeitgeist. After all, architecture is not a direct one-to-one translation of the care vision into bricks and concrete, but rather an opportunity to rethink the provision of services to people with a mental disability again and again, depending on the situation.

The project documentation is followed by a number of essays that focus on the various aspects of design at Monnikenheide and also situate them within a broader context of architecture culture in Flanders.

My text, *Living with a Disability: A Typological Overview*, shows how architectural typology and spatial setting in the various homes at Monnikenheide are deployed as a key in the quest for inclusion of people with mental disabilities. The architectural production presents itself as an ongoing variation on the theme of inclusion, with houses first on the estate and later also in the village. Inclusion is thus conceived as a dynamic process within the functioning of the care centre and in the life of its residents.

In the essay *At Home in the Care Centre: A Look Inside,* Fredie Floré goes over some central practices in recent homes at Monnikenheide, in terms of both collectivity (including entering and eating) and individuality (the bedroom). Less obvious places, which are often forgotten, are also discussed, such as the work area and bathroom, which are therefore all the more charged with ideological stipulations and uses. The design of these functions in a house therefore eminently translates the ambition to provide persons with disabilities with a dignified home.

In *Architecture of Presence,* Heleen Verheyden discusses the socio-spatial dimension of architectural production in Monnikenheide. A critical approach to the programme of inclusion in architecture leads the author to advocate a politics of presence, where 'caring' becomes a radical statement. In this light, Verheyden presents Monnikenheide as a unique example of how architecture enables persons with disabilities to be accepted as part of society as a matter of course.

The essay *Caring for the Landscape of Care*, written by Vjera Sleutel and myself addresses a theme that is present rather implicitly in the architectural history of Monnikenheide. From the beginning, the ambition to allow

4. Paul and Wivina Demeester-De Meyer at the opening of the exhibition *Open Oproep. 20 jaar architectuur in publieke opdracht* in Vandenhove Centrum, Ghent, 2019. © Katrijn Van Giel and Team Flemish Governement Architect Archives

people with disabilities to enjoy the right to territoriality was the occasion for extensive management and spontaneous use of the woods. Today, we can see how the new climate regime has brought the landscape to the fore and how the care institution has been compelled to work, through punctual interventions, towards a comprehensive vision of nature conservation.

The essay *Architecture That Makes People More Beautiful* by Sofie De Caigny situates the significance of Monnikenheide in Flemish architecture culture, more specifically in the long search for quality care architecture. The author outlines the fundamental role of Wivina Demeester, founder and first director of Monnikenheide, in the growing attention paid to care within architecture culture. The genealogy is based on a study of how care architecture was published in Flemish architectural media and how the theme became inscribed in policy in the 2000s.

The book concludes with *Vivre, C'est Faire Vivre*, in which Thomas Vanderveken sketches the biography of Wivina and Paul Demeester. The leitmotif of his homage is the conversation he had with Wivina Demeester on the television programme *Alleen Elvis blijft bestaan* (Only Elvis Survives), where the guest gives us an insight into her world through self-selected film clips. Among other things, a documentary about Charlotte Perriand and the theatre performance of Ayn Rand's *The Fountainhead* provide clues to the social context in which Monnikenheide came into being.

Photography receives special attention in this book, which was in part conceived as a picture book. In this way, we want to do justice to the rich architectural production in Monnikenheide's fifty-year history. The projects were documented and published with photographs commissioned by the architects. The images by various photographers are therefore period documents. The first buildings on the estate are documented with images from the Monnikenheide archive.

Since the existing photographs understandably focus on the built object, we asked art photographer Kurt Deruyter to depict the relations between the buildings, paying attention to the residents' use of this green in-between space. His series of images envisage the overwhelming landscape of Monnikenheide as a whole, outlining the common link of nature as a caring environment for the residents. The images suggest human presence without staging it directly.

Our hope is that this publication sparks further research into an unprecedented housing project. Steven's birth was the occasion for a kaleidoscopic search for the normalization of housing for people with mental disabilities. Fifty years later, Monnikenheide is a life-size architectural statement about the place of these people in society. The collection of houses was not conceived on the basis of one design idea intended to provide universal happiness, but is the result of changing needs and desires, not only among target groups but also over the course of a lifetime. This motive brings us back to Steven, now in his 50s and struggling with dementia, and who, after a period of independent living in Huis aan de Kerk and work in the sheltered workshop Stroom in Merksem, returned to the warmth of the family home.

5. Wivina Demeester with the first Flemish Government Architects, from left to right: Stefan Devoldere, Marcel Smets, Peter Swinnen, Leo Van Broeck and b0b Van Reeth, 2019. © Dries Luyten

1. This introduction draws on research conducted in collaboration with Vjera Sleutel (BAVO) and consisting of, among others, interviews with the initiator Wivina Demeester, technical director Kris De Koninck and all the architects involved. In this book, we use the name Wivina Demeester, as she gained political prominence under this name. By mutual consent, the maiden name is mentioned only occasionally.
2. Lecture by Wivina Demeester at the symposium *Adieu aan het beddenhuis*, organized at Museum Dr. Guislain in Ghent by Museum Dr. Guislain, the Flanders Architecture Institute and the Faculty of Architecture KU Leuven on 24 September 2019. See the report by Vjera Sleutel: https://www.vai.be/nieuws/verslag-studienamiddag-adieu-aan-het-beddenhuis (last accessed January 12, 2023). A short version of the speech was published as an opinion in the special issue of *A+* devoted to care architecture: Wivina Demeester, 'Opinie', *A+ Architecture in Belgium* 283 (April-May 2020), 7.
3. The history of Monnikenheide is documented in: Wivina Demeester-De Meyer, Kris De Koninck and Johan Vermeeren, eds., *Monnikenheide '40'* (Zoersel: vzw Monnikenheide, 2014).
4. Cornelis B. Bakker and Marianne K. Bakker-Rabdau, *No Trespassing! Explorations in Human Territoriality* (San Francisco: Chandler & Sharp, 1973).
5. Unlike at L'Arche, when the first permanent residence was set up at Monnikenheide, the choice was made not to have staff live in. See 'The First Settlement' in this book, 75-76.
6. Michael Speaks, 'Design Intelligence', in *Constructing a New Agenda*, ed. A. K. Sykes (New York: Princeton Architectural Press, 2010), 204–15.
7. The history of the Flemish Government Architect is described in: Marc Santens and Jan De Zutter, *Het Vlaams Bouwmeesterschap 1999-2005* (Antwerp: Houtekiet, 2008). On 17 March 2022, Inge Vervotte took up the torch from Wivina Demeester as president of the board of directors of the Flanders Architecture Institute: https://www.vai.be/nieuws/wivina-demeester-geeft-fakkel-door-aan-inge-vervotte-als-voorzitter-vlaams-architectuurinstituut (last accessed January 12, 2023).
8. Monnikenheide-Spectrum has been headed by managing director Johan Vermeeren and finance director Kris De Koninck since 2020.

LIVING WITH A DISABILITY
A TYPOLOGICAL OVERVIEW
Gideon Boie

The right to territoriality (a space of one's own) is the basic idea with which Monnikenheide gives shape to the inclusion of people with a mental disability.[1] In the early 1970s, people with a mental disability were still often accommodated in psychiatric environments. In response, Wivina and Paul Demeester went in search of an adapted spatial setting in the typical suburban landscape of Zoersel.[2] The woody area provided a safe operating base for later setting up residential projects in the village and the surrounding subdivision.

The right to territoriality also translated into the ambition to normalize housing. To this day, the typical design of hospitals continues to be reflected in the housing of people with disabilities. In contrast, over the years Monnikenheide has experimented with new typologies for small-scale residential care and normalized living.[3] These are houses that are indeed arranged to provide the necessary care or at least support, but which still comply with the general housing ideal.

Combine these two principles with a client that commissions different architects for each project and what you get is a range of unique building projects at Monnikenheide. Other architects have other affinities and build on each other's insights. The architectural history of Monnikenheide therefore embodies a wealth of design knowledge about inclusion and the normalization of housing for people with disabilities.[4] In the following chapter, we provide a brief typological overview.[5]

FAMILY-SIZED SUPPORTED-LIVING RESIDENCES

The story begins with the short-stay home, designed by Bruno Boulanger in 1970 and which still functions today as the main building with a residential programme and administrative offices. The 'short-stay home', as it was called on the plans, was intended to accommodate people with disabilities for a limited period of time in order to relieve the burden on their families. Originally, the building consisted of identical pavilions, constructed using the prefabricated Danilith system and connected by a single corridor. The middle pavilion was meant for the communal services. On either side of it was a separate pavilion for boys and for girls. The architectural typology shows Monnikenheide's ambition to work with family-sized supported-living units, small groups of eight residents who live almost independently. Each pavilion had two rooms for three or four persons and two living rooms at the end walls, a far cry from the classic typology of hospital dormitories.

The focus on small-scale units is recognizable in all later developments at Monnikenheide, each time in varying forms. For example, Monnikenbos (1980) was designed by Luc Van den Broeck as a clustered house for permanent residence. With its brick walls, sloping roofs and small verandas, the building has the appearance of a scout hut. The architectural style hardly differs from

1. Former entry to the short-stay home – Bruno Boulanger © Monnikenheide Archives

private houses of the time. The complex consists of three houses for seven residents, connected by a central pavilion that also functioned as a general entrance, community room and sports hall. The same architectural style is used in Monnikenhuis (1980), a home for four residents who live together independently. Werkhuis (1985) also shows a similar style in a slightly anthroposophical tradition, although this is a non-residential building.

The focus on small-scale, family-sized supported-living units is even more evident in the renovation and extension of the short-stay home. The new complex is informally called 'het hoofdgebouw' (the main building) (2003) and combines a residential programme on the ground floor with the administrative offices in an annexe built on the roof. In Jo Peeters's design, the capacity of the short-stay home is reduced to one resident group of eight people per pavilion, with living rooms on one side of the corridor and individual bedrooms on the other. At the end, the pavilions were given a glass extension containing the living rooms that look out onto the central alley. The complex was extended by one pavilion, which has exactly the same form as the previous one. The backbone that connects all the pavilions was also opened up with large windows. Opposite the new entrance to the main building, a laundry and a therapy pool were built, which, as separate facilities, encourage the use of the outdoor space.

The same deepening of the family-sized supported-living homes can be seen in the dismantling and reuse of Monnikenbos, a design by UR architects. The renovation was completed in 2020, although the design process had already started in 2012. The central entrance pavilion that used to give access to the three pavilions was removed and the communal functions were housed in a separate building.[1] The intervention reverses the circulation logic. The three pavilions are now even more closely related to each other. The shared space is no longer hidden behind doors, but serves as an open common courtyard where the various groups of residents meet.[6] The intervention also improved the way the pavilions function as homes because they can be identified as such, having, among other things, their own front door and a small garden.

The focus on small-scale housing is a constant in all subsequent building projects at Monnikenheide, such as Monnikenhuis, built in 1980 and later renovated and renamed Zonnebloem (2010). The recent building De Eiken (2016), also designed by UR architects (then under the corporate name TV Nikolaas Vande Keere and Regis Verplaetse), added an extra fifth pavilion to the backbone of the main building, with a façade that suggests it is the end of the line. Its position at the end of the corridor makes it possible to situate the shared spaces (sitting room, dining room, kitchen) in the middle of the house and to provide on two sides a short corridor with rooms. The typology of small-scale housing is clearly reflected in the development of sheltered housing outside the main domain of Monnikenheide. This brings us to the next topic of inclusion: spatial planning.

2. Monnikenbos – Luc Van den Broeck
© Monnikenheide Archives
3. Huis aan de Voorne – Huiswerk architecten
© Niels Donckers

AN INCLUSIVE SPACE

The architecture of Monnikenheide is, besides typology, also about the use of the spatial environment for the inclusion of people with a mental and physical disability. The idea was to free people with disabilities from the logic of the institution and to situate them in the everyday urban and social fabric, more specifically the typical suburban reality of Flanders. Monnikenheide was built as an open domain in the woods, on the edge of a subdivision, just outside the centre of Zoersel. Pavilions are literally spread across the domain, as if it were a small subdivision itself. The first settlements consist of the short-stay home (1973), the staff building (1973, later adapted for permanent residence and renamed Rode Roos), Monnikenbos (1980), Monnikenhuis (1980) and Werkhuis (1985), supplemented by an animal pasture, sports fields and later a therapy pool and a laundry. The scattered settlement on the grounds encourages residents to make use of the woods, the neighbourhood and the village centre according to their possibilities, with or without supervision.

Full immersion in the typical Flemish settlement pattern is achieved when homes are built in the village itself. In its attempt to meet the specific care needs of its residents, Monnikenheide has played a pioneering role in the typology of sheltered housing. The first experiment in independent living for people with disabilities took place at the Monnikenhuis residence. Although the location of Monnikenheide is already inclusive, the setting ultimately limits the possibilities for some residents, especially in the area of self-reliance. The four residents were therefore moved to an existing house in the ribbon subdivision of the river Voorne, on the corner of Langebaan, the street that leads to Monnikenheide. This initiative sowed the seed for the later Huis aan de Voorne (2003), designed by Dirk Somers (at the time associated with the agency Huiswerk architecten by Erik Wieërs, today with Bovenbouw Architectuur). The house has a capacity for eight residents, the idea being that they organize their work and living independently. Care workers are only available to help at breakfast and in the evenings. During the day, the residents set off to work in social enterprises in Antwerp or at the Werkhuis at Monnikenheide.

The location of the home for sheltered housing offers the residents direct proximity to social facilities (bakeries, grocery shops, bus stops, etc.) and thus supports their participation in the village community. At the same time, the community can serve as a support network for people with disabilities. The next building project was therefore developed on the village square itself, as if it were a small provocation. Huis aan de Kerk (2004), designed by Johan De Coster (at the time associated as a trainee with Mys-Bomans architecten, today Vermeiren De Coster Architecten), is in the heart of the village, directly opposite the main church and the primary school. Thanks to the central location, the residents can build up a relational network, as a result of which the villagers unconsciously care for the people with disabilities – for example, by helping them cross the street, by giving them change when they pay at the grocery shop, when they board the bus to Antwerp, etc.

4. Main building – Architectuurgroep Jo Peeters © IRS Studiebureau
5. Huis aan de Kerk – Vermeiren De Coster Architecten © Niels Donckers

CONVERGENCES

Architectural typology and spatial setting do not operate in isolation, but rather along interwoven lines of development. The building projects for sheltered housing are not only about the spatial setting. They also show unusual variations in the typology of a care home, particularly in the division between private and communal space. In Huis aan de Voorne, for example, individual rooms were conceived as studios with their own lounge and kitchenette, while the communal area was given fairly minimal furnishings. The most important collective space is a stately atrium with an open staircase that continues into the kitchen, which has a dining area and a view of the garden. The focus in the design was on the individual room as a studio that enables the resident to be self-sufficient. It is only later that the atrium was furnished as a living room with sofas.

The internal logic of Huis aan de Kerk, by contrast, is more like that of a classic house. The emphasis is on the living room and the kitchen, which together serve as a cosy and familiar communal space. From the living room, an open staircase leads to the individual rooms upstairs, which are still conceived as spacious studios with private sanitary facilities, but without a fully equipped kitchenette. The intention of the redistribution was to resemble a family home as much as possible and as such to normalize the care home.

The typological innovations in the sheltered housing projects subsequently recur in the new construction on the main estate of Monnikenheide. Huis aan 't Laar (2013), designed by Peter Swinnen (at the time associated with 51N4E, today with CRIT. architects), converts the typology of protected living into a detached house in the woods. Huis aan 't Laar is used by people with higher care needs who are still able to live independently. The house brings together two groups of eight people around a helical staircase so that the groups are in constant relation to each other but never actually touch. The position of the living room with a dining room and kitchen behind a door allows the residents to go to their individual rooms without having to encounter other residents or staff. The rooms are conceived as small L-shaped studios with two or even three windows, each room enjoying different views and varying incidence of light. The bathroom is located in the kink, so that the studio has different angles and sides and the resident can decide on the openness of the room. A strong contrast with the unrestricted view in the classic hospital room.

The same distribution of space comes to the fore in the construction of Villa Kameleon (2021), designed by FELT architecture & design. The sheltered house is situated in a subdivision a stone's throw from the Monnikenheide estate. The house presents itself as a detached villa and brings together eight L-shaped rooms in a hexagonal ground plan. The central lobby is again a rather bare circulation space that allows the residents to reach their private rooms without having to pass through communal living or dining rooms, so that they enjoy privacy and independence in their daily comings and goings. The large rooms have multiple windows that bring daylight even into the bathrooms.

6. Huis aan 't Laar – 51N4E © Filip Dujardin
7. De Eiken – UR architects © Tim Van de Velde

AN OPEN END

Giving people with disabilities the right to territoriality prompted the search for forms of housing that blend into the typical suburban subdivision landscape in Zoersel. The establishment of Monnikenheide is therefore an obvious negation of the age-old logic of separation that underlies care institutions and their stigmatizing housing models.[7] The marvel is that the history of Monnikenheide does not end there, but instead unfolds as a successive 'negation of negation'.[8] The building projects constantly stretch and rethink the territorial scope of the residents, responding to their various needs and desires.

The short history of architectural production at Monnikenheide thus demonstrates a dynamic logic of inclusion for people with mental and physical disabilities. The great variety of housing solutions in Monnikenheide lies beyond good and evil. It is not a question of one project working better than another. What matters is the diversification of the housing supply for people with disabilities and the ability to adapt to changing needs, not only between different target groups but also over the span of a lifetime.

8. Monnikenbos – UR architects © Michiel De Cleene
9. Villa Kameleon – FELT architecture & design © Stijn Bollaert

1 In an interview with the author, Wivina Demeester refers to the territorial approach of Cornelis B. Bakker and Marianne K. Bakker-Rabdau as the motivation for the family-sized supported-living units, 28 May 2021. See: C.B. Bakker and M.K. Bakker-Rabdau, *No Trespassing! Explorations in Human Territoriality* (San Francisco: Chandler & Sharp, 1973).

2 Wivina Demeester, lecture at the symposium *Adieu aan het beddenhuis*, organized by the Museum Dr. Guislain in Ghent on 24 September 2019. See the report by Vjera Sleutel on the website of the Flanders Architecture Institute: https://www.vai.be/nieuws/verslag-studienamiddag-adieu-aan-het-beddenhuis. A short version of the speech was published in the issue of *A+* on care architecture: Wivina Demeester, 'Opinie', *A+ Architecture in Belgium* 283 (April-May 2020), 7.

3 Rethinking the architecture of the hospital as a model for residential care was the topic of the symposium *Adieu aan het beddenhuis*. See also: Gideon Boie, 'Sleutelen aan het beddenhuis', *A+ Architecture in Belgium* 283 (April-May 2020), 42-47.

4 Michael Speaks argued how 'design intelligence' is constructed through everyday 'chatter' rather than fixed typologies and heroic forms. See: Michael Speaks, 'Design Intelligence', in *Constructing a New Agenda*, ed. A. Krista Sykes (New York: Princeton Architectural Press, 2010), 204–15.

5 This article is based on research carried out in collaboration with Vjera Sleutel (BAVO) and constructed out of interviews with the architects and clients involved. An early version of the text was published by *E-Flux* under the title *Models of Inclusion* in the Sick Architecture series edited by Nick Axel, Beatriz Colomina and Nikolaus Hirsch (13 June 2022).

6 The intervention was developed as a prototype by UR architects in the context of mental healthcare in the Netherlands. See: UR architects, *De Psychiatrische Kliniek Ontmanteld, studie voor het Stimuleringsfonds Architectuur* (Rotterdam, 2009). The study was the basis for the exhibition *De toekomst van het gesticht* in the *Jonge makers, denkers, dromers* series of the Flanders Architecture Institute (26 September–29 October 2012).

7 Michel Foucault argued how the programme of resocialization for psychiatric patients in William Tuke's The Retreat was, after all, a strange thing considering the fact that we first separate these people. Although justified as a critique, the argument does not take into account that separation might be necessary in some delicate care programmes. See: Michel Foucault, *Madness and Civilization: A History of Insanity in the Age of Reason* (Tavistock Publications, 1961; Abingdon: Routlegde, 2001), 229-264.

8 Slavoj Zizek argued how the Hegelian synthesis is not so much a peaceful reconciliation of opposites as the 'negation of (the first) negation'. See: Slavoj Zizek, *The Ticklish Subject* (London: Verso, 1999), 72.

Jos. DEMEESTER   LEDEBERG-GENT.
                                                  BRUSSELSESTEENWEG 37

    Ondergetekenden Demeester Jozef en Jacobs Rach_el verklaren over te dragen bij schenking, waarvan de kosten aan de genieters, te Zoersel in de Sectie C genoemd "De Schaapskooi":

1/ het perceel 231 h zijnde mastbos groot 9720 m2 aan de V.Z.W. Monnikenheide, waarvan beheerders Paul en Wivina Demeester De Meyer, met de bedoeling er door de verkrijger een kort-verblijf-home voor mentaal gehandikapte kinderen te zien oprichten en in stand te houden. Gemeld goed zou terugkomen aan de schenkers bij het ophouden van dit vooruitzicht, onvergoed en op kosten van de V.Z.W.
Het goed is begrensd op de gehele Westkant door gracht en uitweg, die voor de helft blijft toebehoren aan de schenkers.

2/ het deel van het perceel 240 C bosgrond op de oostkant gelegen en nevens genoemde uitweg met aan de voorkant (NO) een breedte van 70 meter en in de diepte langs de uitweg 72 m. samen groot: 5040 m2 aan Demeester Paul en De Meyer Wivina thans wonende Balderij 3 Tielen. Moest wat de diepte van 72 m. betreft het houten huisje en aanhorigheid binnen deze grens vallen dan blijft het gebruik hiervan onvergoed en levenslang ten-voordele van de schenkers.

                Gent 24 juni 1970

Donation deed for two plots of land in the Schaapskooi in Zoersel, one plot to vzw Monnikenheide and a second to Paul and Wivina Demeester-De Meyer, signed by Jozef Demeester and Rachel Jacobs (24 June, 1970).
© Demeester Archives

Laying of the foundation stone of Monnikenbos on 5 May 1979. On the left next to Wivina Demeester is Bert Hertecant, chairman of the board of directors. On the far right: Belgian prime minister Wilfried Martens. Far left, with hands in pockets: resident Jan Daemen. Handyman Marcel Van Dijck looks on with arms crossed. © Monnikenheide Archives

AT HOME IN THE CARE CENTRE
A LOOK INSIDE
Fredie Floré

That architecture should make people more beautiful is a basic premise of Monnikenheide. The interior is perhaps the place par excellence where this ambition can be realized. It is the place where users interact directly with the spatial conditions of a building and where they can experience the architecture in all its sensorial power. Buildings are multisensory structures, as Finnish architect Juhani Pallasmaa has explained.[1] Especially inside, perceptions of sound, texture, smell, light, heat, mass and scale are intense. In residential and care architecture, these experiences have a direct impact on the extent to which residents or other users can feel secure, valued, recognized, supported or reassured – all conditions that can allow people to feel happier and therefore more 'beautiful'.

The choice of scale and typology for the collective residence sets the tone for the experience of the interiors of Monnikenheide, regardless of how diverse the architecture of the individual houses may be. While various aspects unmistakably remind us that we are in a care environment – sturdy, washable furniture, floor and wall coverings that can withstand intensive use, large bathrooms with adapted sanitary appliances – it is the impressions that are related to living or that appeal to living that predominate. Huis aan de Voorne, De Eiken, Monnikenbos, Huis aan 't Laar and Villa Kameleon – the projects discussed in this text – are residences that each in their own way make room for domestic experiences and the attribution of meaning. Not of an individual, a couple or a family, but of a group of eight to nine individuals and the care staff who support and guide them in their daily lives.

ENTERING AND CONNECTING

Entering the collective residences at Monnikenheide is meaningful in itself. Although the main building with its central reception desk is the one that most recalls a traditional care institution, this is rarely the case with the other houses. The three residential units of Monnikenbos, for example, are opened up through fully glazed entrance doors from a newly created outdoor area. Even before visitors enter, large windows provide generous views of the residents' communal rooms. A functional entrance gives direct access to the horizontal backbone of the house: a wide corridor, if you can even call it that, which practically all the rooms give onto, including those on the first floor. Whoever enters here reaches the collective heart of the house without detours and immediately becomes a part of it.

1. Monnikenbos – UR architects © Michiel De Cleene

Other houses focus less directly on community life, but celebrate the potential of connectedness just as much, although in different ways. At Huis aan de Voorne, from under the covered porch at the front door, you step straight into the heart of the house via a small entrance: a central hallway, several storeys high, which virtually all the rooms and also the stairs give onto. Whoever wants to retreat to his or her studio can do so without many detours, but it is also possible to reconnect rapidly from every floor, at least in visual or auditory terms. In the case of Huis aan 't Laar and Villa Kameleon, the act of entering is a little more stretched out or phased – in the former, through a corridor that is an extension of the access path winding through the trees; in the latter, through an in-house outdoor portal, a small outdoor room, preceding the actual entrance. But in both cases, the emphasis is again on the possibility and importance of connection, in two variants rendered by a centrally positioned staircase. In Huis aan 't Laar, it is a double open spiral staircase, one for each group of residents housed in the building. At Villa Kameleon, it is a single, fluidly designed monolithic staircase. Both connecting elements and the daily movements that take place on them are gracefully lit by a skylight.

VARIATIONS ON A FAMILIAR DOMESTIC FORMULA

The fact that the houses are immediately recognizable as a house is primarily due to the way in which the communal living areas are designed. In most cases, for example in Huis aan 't Laar, they accommodate a combination of functions that are instantly familiar: a dining area, an open kitchen, a sitting area and a desk or home office. Today, the constellation reads like a domestic formula that is familiar to Flanders, even though its use and appropriation is to some extent unique.

For example, the kitchen is not the place where meals are prepared three times a day. After all, in the main building there is a large kitchen that caters for the residents of Monnikenheide. The significance of the kitchens in the homes at Monnikenheide, as in many more conventional homes today, lies just as much in their visual value. Together with the dining areas, they form a recognizable and familiar setting where meals are eaten at more or less fixed times every day and where other activities can take place in-between. In addition, the kitchens make simple household activities and occasional cooking possible – baking pancakes, for example. Their open character means that anyone who wants to can be involved, in whatever way they want.

In this respect, the communal kitchen in Villa Kameleon is particularly inviting. It was given a central place in the living area and is equipped with a long kitchen island that can accommodate several people, as the designers

2. Villa Kameleon – FELT architecture & design © Stijn Bollaert
3. Huis aan 't Laar – 51N4E © Filip Dujardin

also highlighted in their plans. The cupboards are made of a flat green sheet material that harmonizes with the range of green tiles that characterize Villa Kameleon both on the outside and inside. The wooded surroundings, which appear particularly close in the kitchen thanks to two large sliding windows with green awnings, complete the colour palette and link the visual play in good weather with the sound of rustling leaves.

 A collective sitting room is another recurring domestic ingredient in the Monnikenheide homes. In the architectural plans, we can recognize this part of the building by the sketched-in seats and coffee table, but what the drawings usually show less clearly is that there is generally also a small desk in this space. This is a modest worktable for the Monnikenheide care staff, sometimes supplemented by a rack or cabinet for folders or other paperwork. Instead of setting up a separate office for administrative work and thus articulating the difference between residents and care providers, in almost all houses, with the exception of the residents' private rooms or studios, maximum use is made of the shared space. Some architectural projects nevertheless provide a specific place for the home office. In the residential units of Monnikenbos, for example, the end point of the central corridor is designed for this purpose, a handy niche that immediately adjoins the communal seating area. In other houses, the workplace consists of a simple combination of table, cupboard and windowsill in the middle or at the edge of the living space – a scene that can also be found in many living rooms in Flanders, especially with the rise in home working.[2]

 The shared or collective interiors of the residential entities have a recognizably domestic character, but extra care, protection or support are an intrinsic part of them. This is particularly evident in some communal bathrooms equipped with adapted sanitary fittings. This is the case, for example, in De Eiken, a new construction for eight severely invalid residents whose shape is literally attuned to a series of neighbouring oak trees. Unlike in most other houses, the residents do not have a private bathroom in their bedroom, but a spacious washroom at the end of the common corridor. The room is unmistakably designed for people with special needs. The appliances and the dimensions leave no doubt about this. At the same time, the care with which the interior has been designed connects the room to the whole of the house. Like all the other rooms, the bathroom has a large window that looks out onto one of the oaks. The fresh green vinyl floor covering that can be found throughout the house flows here almost seamlessly into a variant with an anti-slip surface. The walls are covered with the same Parisian metro tiles as in the open kitchen. This bathroom – in itself a highly regulated room – has not been designed as a medicalized unit, but as a place for physical care and well-being within the architectural concept of the house. Sanitary rooms usually remain underexposed in debates about architecture, but they are often particularly significant and ideologically charged spaces, as architectural historian Barbara Penner explains.[3] In the case of Monnikenheide, the way they are designed is perhaps the prime expression of the ambition to give people in need of care both a home and place that are comfortable and dignified in the world.

4. Villa Kameleon – FELT architecture & design © Stijn Bollaert
5. Huis aan 't Laar – 51N4E © Filip Dujardin

PERSONALIZED SPACE

In addition to the shared interiors, the individual rooms help to shape the idea of the house. In the Monnikenheide housing entities discussed here, these rooms take on various forms, from a compact bedroom with a washbasin and a few built-in wardrobes (De Eiken) to larger studios with their own bathroom and kitchenette (Huis aan de Voorne). As with any new or designed house, they are conceived in the hope of them becoming a personalized space, where the resident takes control and feels secure – secure enough to face the world outside the room and the house. After all, a house that is only a nest is unhealthy or unliveable, says philosopher Bart Verschaffel.[4] Change, movement, connection with the outside world – made possible in architecture with elements such as the window, the door and the threshold – are also essential parts of the construction of domesticity.

The extent to which and the way in which Monnikenheide residents themselves actively contribute to transforming the private room or studio into a personal nest varies. One of the most striking forms of personalization is clearly orchestrated collectively. There is always a picture of the resident next to or on the door of the private room or studio. The photographs clearly mark the threshold or transition between the shared and the private space. Inside the rooms and studios, there is room for the resident's own furniture and belongings – material objects that, according to anthropologist Daniel Miller, usually present themselves to us as a representation of both the world outside the private domain and the way in which the resident appropriates that world.[5] The architecture of Monnikenheide's individual rooms and studios does not form a neutral canvas for these elements but rather facilitates and invites domestication in simple ways. In several houses, the window plays a central role in this. At both Huis aan 't Laar and Villa Kameleon, for example, most if not all the rooms were given views in two directions – something made possible by the bent shape of the façades. The double view of the surroundings and the varying light incidence that goes with it introduce a subtle form of zoning into the interior that can be filled in at will or with the help of loved ones.

The houses of Monnikenbos follow a different model. Here, the ground floor rooms do not have a façade with window openings, but a fully glazed extension with its own exterior door. This is a consequence of the design decision to give the original care homes from the 1980s (which served as the starting point for this renovation project) a new, partially glazed roof and also new façades. This gave the existing individual rooms a sun-drenched extension – an intervention that seems to refer to the much-discussed renovation of the residential tower in the Grand Parc quarter in Bordeaux by architects Lacaton & Vassal, Druot and Hutin in 2017. But while the new interior terraces in Bordeaux are connected as much as possible to the existing living spaces and thus make them more spacious, the added spaces of the rooms in Monnikenbos are rather separately articulated interiors. In other words, the rooms have two parts. The first is contained within the volume of the original building, whose red brick wall has been preserved. There is room for a single

6. De Eiken – UR architects © Michiel De Cleene

bed, a washbasin and in some cases a built-in wardrobe. The second part (the extension) presents itself above all as a place to be filled in freely, which can be closed off from the first part of the room with a simple curtain. The limited size of the extension makes the space manageable and sheltered. At the same time, the generous glazing provides direct contact with the green surroundings and the play of light that goes with it. The way in which several of the current residents use the added spaces – as a place to listen to music, keep photos of family members or friends, hang drawings, collect personal objects or simply hang around – underlines the potential of these rooms as both a nest and a safe starting point for interaction with the outside world, whatever form it may take.

INTERIOR IN CONTEXT

The architecture of the collective houses of Monnikenheide generates interiors from which the world can be explored and inhabited. The fact that various functions that are not directly related to the usual residential programme but are essential for the care, support or well-being of the residents are housed in separate buildings on the site, underlines the character of the houses as residential entities. For example, there is a workhouse with various workshops where residents can work or a stand-alone bathhouse with a therapy bath. Anyone who goes there or engages in other activities briefly leaves their own nest and comes home again a little later. These repetitive actions help to keep the meaning of the house alive for its residents and in the foreground. The care facilities are always unmistakably present, but they are embedded as a matter of course in a whole that can still be described first and foremost as a residential environment.

7. Huis aan 't Laar – 51N4E © Filip Dujardin
8. Monnikenbos – UR architects © Michiel De Cleene

1 Juhani Pallasmaa, 'An Architecture of the Seven Senses', in *Toward a New Interior: An Anthology of Interior Design Theory*, ed. Lois Weinthal (New York: Princeton Architectural Press, 2011), 40–49.
2 For reflections on the long-standing phenomenon of the home office, see e.g. Akiko Bush, *Geography of Home: Writings on Where We Live* (New York: Princeton Architectural Press, 1999), 81–91.
3 Barbara Penner, *Bathroom* (London: Reaktion Books, 2013), 14.
4 Bart Verschaffel, *Van Hermes en Hestia: Teksten over architectuur* (Ghent: A&S/books, 2006), 88.
5 Daniel Miller, 'Behind Closed Doors', in *Home Possessions: Material Culture Behind Closed Doors*, ed. Daniel Miller (Oxford/New York: Berg, 2001), 1–19.

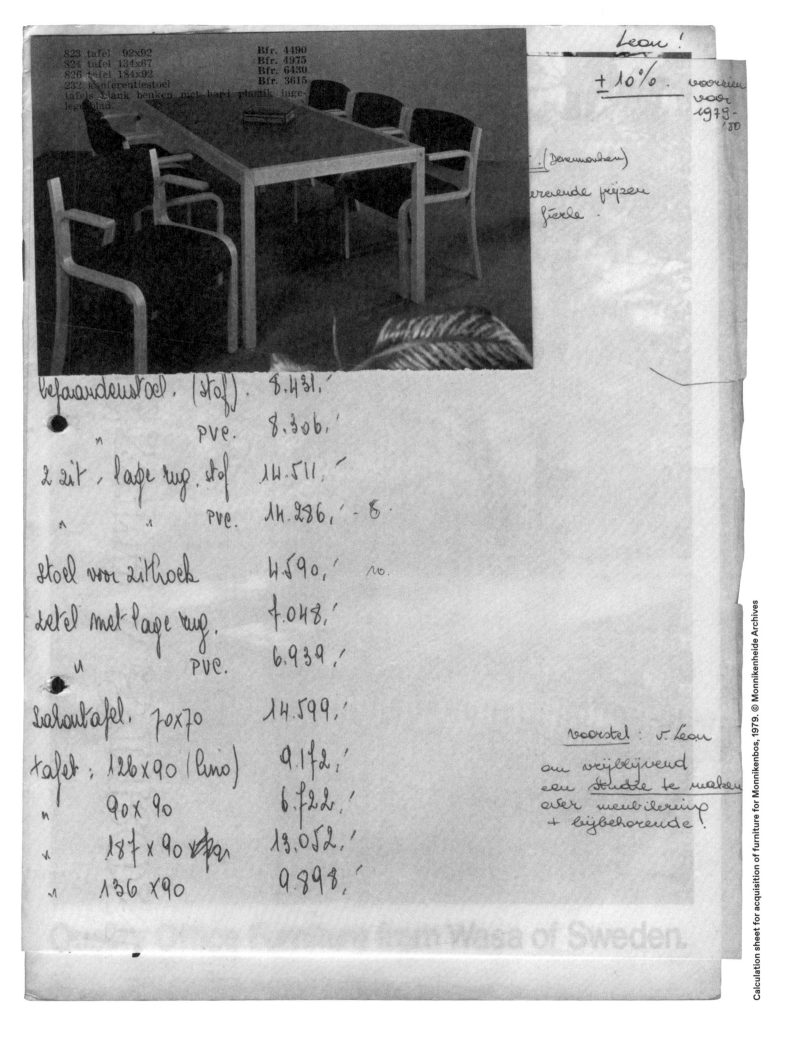

Calculation sheet for acquisition of furniture for Monnikenbos, 1979. © Monnikenheide Archives

VIJFENDERTIG BEDDEN

De bedoeling is op dit terrein vijf afzonderlijke geprefabriceerde paviljoenen op te trekken, die elk onderdak zouden kunnen verlenen aan... Voor het bouwen wacht men enkel op een besluit van de minister voor het verlenen van een Staatstoelage, die tot 60 t.h. van de bouwkosten kan bedragen.

"Ons land telt 50.000 zwaar mentaal gehandicapten"
"Laatste nieuws" 29.10.70

Kortverblijf voor mentaal gehandicapten

Wanneer eerste steen voor Monnikenheide?

"Gazet van Antwerpen" 29.10.70

Ouders kunnen dan ook eens echt vakantie nemen

"Standaard"

Psycholoog Bert Hertecant, voorzitter van de raad van beheer, en mevrouw De Meyer, sekretaris kunnen morgen meteen de eerste steen van «Monnikenheide» leggen. Met de bouwwerken zelf is ... , maar zij wachten op de principiële toezegging van subsidies van het ministerie van Volksgezondheid. Het spreekt vanzelf dat de uitbatingslasten van een dergelijk centrum niet draaglijk zijn wanneer de staat niet helpt.

Bert Hertecant meent dat in ons land een dergelijk centrum per provincie zou moeten gebouwd worden. In de begroting van Volksgezondheid staat reeds drie jaar nakaar de principiële beslissing ingeschreven om dergelijke initiatieven te steunen. Tot nog toe vaardigde de minister geen uitvoeringsbesluiten uit.

Kort-verblijfhome te Zoersel wacht op uitvoeringsbesluit

de regering moet nu handelen!

Het beginsel van het kort-verblijfcentrum is in de Belgische wetgeving opgenomen: de Wet op het Fonds voor medische, sociale en pedagogische zorg voor gehandicapten voorziet de terugbetaling van de onderhoudsprijs per dag en op de begroting van het Ministerie van Volksgezondheid komt sinds verschillende jaren een post voor met betrekking op kort-verblijf-centra.

Wat wij bijgevolg vragen aan de Regering: dat zij zo spoedig mogelijk een besluit zou uitvaardigen voor de erkenning en voor het bouwen en uitrusten van kort-verblijf-centra. Tevens dat de werkingskosten voldoende zouden zijn om deze centra toe te laten op behoorlijke wijze te functioneren.

besluit

* In het Vlaamse landsgedeelte is er een behoefte aan een kort-verblijf-centrum: tot dusver bestaat er geen;

* het initiatief te Zoersel is loyaal pluralistisch: het verdient bijgevolg de steun van de gehele bevolking;

* het principe van het kort-verblijf-centrum is in de wetgeving opgenomen: het is bijgevolg mogelijk spoedig te handelen.

R. VAN DER KELEN

Informatie kan bekomen worden bij Mevr. ir. Wivina Demeester-De Meyer, Balderij 3, 2450 Tielen.

"De Bond" 26.11.70

Om naar uit te kijken

Zo groeide de idee van *Monnikenheide*. De schenking van een flinke lap grond te Zoersel (niet ver van Antwerpen, in een nog gezonde dennebossen-streek) was de eerste stap om de droom werkelijkheid te maken. Intussen werden nog vele stappen gezet. Er kwam een beheerraad, een aangroeiende ... helpen... En nu is het zover: dat alleen nog gewacht wordt op het uitvoeringsbesluit, dat de gedeeltelijke subsidiëring van de bouwkosten zal vrijmaken. (Volksgezondheid voorziet sedert drie jaar in haar buitengewone begroting, toelagen voor dergelijke initiatieven. Het KB dat dit moet bekrachtigen, wordt spoedig verwacht).

Nieuwe home gehandikapten te Zoersel

BRUSSEL (eigen berichtgeving) — Op een perskonferentie te Brussel werd gistermiddag meegedeeld dat de vereniging «Monnikenheide» v.z.w. werd opgericht om te doel te Zoersel nabij Antwerpen een home voor beperkt verblijf voor mentaal gehandikapten op te richten. De gronden midden bossen gelegen, zijn reeds beschikbaar, de bouwvergunning werd toegekend en de subsidiëring vanwege het ministerie van Volksgezondheid...

instellingen zijn hopeloos verouderde oplossingen.

Kortverblijf-Home voor mentaal Gehandicapte Kinderen in de maak

„Monnikenheide" wordt te Zoersel opgericht

De jongste jaren hebben verantwoordelijken voor onze nationale gezondheid en het algemeen welzijn, de overheden van alle verantwoordelijkheidskringen meer bewust gemaakt van ... op de begroting. Het enige wat ontbreekt is het uitvoeringsbesluit.

De belofte om deze K.B. deze week nog te laten verschijnen werd alleszins gedaan. Afwachten dus. De staat zou in dat geval voor 60 t.h. bijpassen. Het ontbrekende moet dan uit de traditionele Vlaamse solidariteit en vrijgevigheid bijeengezocht worden.

... voor het verblijf van een mentaal gehandicapt kind worden de ouders, 100 à 150 fr. per dag, en door de Nationale Dienst voor Kinderwelzijn gedeeld.

Wat we vaststaat, afgaande op de beslistheid van de initiatiefnemers op de persconferentie te Brussel waarop zij hun project voorstelden, is, dat door het systeem van prefab-bouw na negen maanden de eerste kinderen zullen opgenomen worden, met of zonder financiële moeilijkheden.

Noteren we nog dat de v.z.w. Monnikenheide uitgaat van een gezond pluralisme zodat er niet met de kinderen en hun ouders om dubieuze redenen gesold wordt.

"Volksgazet" 29.10.70

... toestand van de gehandicapte in ons land, is dat de kinderen heden niet meer in overbevolkte, niet goed uitgeruste psychiatrische inrichtingen worden ondergebracht, maar een opleidingsbehandeling genieten in internaatsverband. De kinderen kunnen dus huiswaarts keren. Een passende hulp en een begeleiding op de weg naar huis is dus nodig. De taak van de ouders is zeer zwaar. Ervaringen in de ons omringende landen (Denemarken, Nederland) hebben die bezwaren weggedacht door een ideale oplossing te geven aan... probleem van de mentaal gehandicapten, nl. de centra voor kort verblijf («short-stay-homes»). In België bestaat een dergelijk initiatief te Mez-sur-Semois). «Monnikenheide» zou de tweede verwezenlijking zijn, de eerste in het Vlaamse landsgedeelte.

VAN 14 DAGEN TOT 3 MAANDEN

De vereniging «Monnikenheide» v.z.w. heeft het plan opgevat om te Zoersel, nabij Antwerpen, een home voor beperkt verblijf voor mentaal gehandicapten op te richten. De gronden midden bossen gelegen zijn reeds beschikbaar, de bouwvergunning werd toegekend en de subsidiëring vanwege het ministerie van Volksgezondheid werd aangevraagd.

Monnikenheide is geen nieuw bedrijf ter bevordering van de economische en sociale welvaart, geen school en geen opleidingscentrum voor verantwoorde vrijetijdsbeste...

"Het Volk" 24.10.70

ARCHITECTURE OF PRESENCE
Heleen Verheyden

Designing for inclusion sounds good: everyone has the right to belong. But the term is rather vague. Inclusion seems to be a catch-all term that makes little distinction between the different domains and spheres of life in which one wants to include people. The magic word 'inclusion' is used for all individuals and groups who are vulnerable due to various circumstances or who face discrimination: 'you are allowed to participate' – and everyone seems to know where you should participate.

This vagueness carries over into the discussion about how we can design for inclusion. There is an epistemological risk that inclusion is reduced to a number of design concepts and that the foundations of equality underlying it are ignored. In this way, the designer often unconsciously maintains a value scale of what constitutes a dignified life and who has the right to participate in society.

Imperialism and neoliberal capitalism have created and justified exclusionary mechanisms based on social class, gender, race, body type or health. This has resulted in deep-seated forms of racism, sexism and ableism (discrimination on the basis of functional disability). People with a disability are often reduced to their identity of care-dependent persons. They are not seen as full-fledged individuals with decision-making rights, and their disability is often viewed from the perspective of independence to be pursued.

Designing for the inclusion of people in need of care is therefore impossible without a critical awareness of deeply rooted inequalities. It requires an awareness of one's own potential as a client and designer to question structural injustices, expose inequalities, negotiate power relations and rewrite the norm. Designing for inclusion must in essence be political and premised on a 'politics of presence', where the physical presence of people in need of care and anti-capitalist role models is in itself a political claim.[1]

Monnikenheide plays an exemplary role in this reflection. The centre shows that designing for the inclusion of people with disabilities goes beyond the application of design concepts and gives rise to a politics of presence by negotiating and claiming the right to exist and the presence of people with disabilities on a daily basis.

THE ILLUSION OF INCLUSION

To arrive at a conscious application of the term 'inclusion', we need to go back to the roots of the word. The term was originally used in the

1. Walter Swennen, *Zij die hier zijn zijn van hier* [Those who are here are from here], 2007, M HKA Collection. © M HKA

medical-social field, which ties it to a specific approach as regards people who are excluded because of their disabilities or capabilities.[2] The same emphasis on combating discrimination of people with a physical disability lies at the basis of 'universal design'. The inclusion of people with disabilities thereby starts from the idea of making differences irrelevant rather than from the idea of closing the gap between people's characteristics and society's norms.[3]

While the philosophy 'whereby it is normal to be different'[4] is valuable in the context of people with physical disabilities, it becomes highly problematic in other contexts, such as the inclusion of the poor or refugees, since it implies that there is no need to change the situation of someone's otherness.[5] Inclusion thus risks becoming a passive and paternalistic endeavour in which inequalities are tacitly accepted.

Within the perspective of inclusion for people with a disability, there is also a need for a more dynamic view of the concept by assuming a developmental perspective.[6] This supposes that a person's social inclusion can improve as their ability to interact with others and participate in activities increases.

Gradually, inclusion became the new paradigm in the care sector and in the migration debate, replacing the increasingly criticized concept of 'integration'. Contrary to integration, which is very coercive and requires adaptation to the prevailing norms of society, inclusion presupposes a two-way street, whereby the sick, vulnerable or discriminated person not only have to adapt to 'us', but we also have to adapt to 'them'. The term 'inclusion', however, possesses the same paternalistic, neocolonial and imperialistic tendency, while passing itself off as humanitarian.

Inclusion assumes that a society allows a marginalized community to take its place in society. This in turn assumes that the society you are referring to is somehow homogeneous, with certain prevailing values, beliefs and cultural behaviours. But this too fosters discrimination, for you assume a normality or homogeneity that does not exist. In this way, you tacitly accept that anyone who cannot be identified with the homogeneous group is not part of society.

POLITICS OF PRESENCE

The vagueness of the concept of 'inclusion' and the tacit acceptance of inequalities it implies often lead to discussions on how we can promote inclusion through architecture and urban design that are beside the point. The debate is often reduced to a search for design concepts and socio-spatial principles that tend to forget the underlying foundations of equality. One of the concepts often used within care architecture is based on a literal spatial translation of inclusion, whereby care architecture must literally be integrated into the city or village.

Often, this idea stems from the conviction that the city offers the most opportunities for development and that people can live more independently there. However, these opportunities for development are based on a neoliberal and capitalist logic: the city is where you can find work, where you can make connections more quickly, in short, where you have more opportunities for growth. Inclusion is thus measured in terms of productivity and the ability to live independently, which is not appropriate for people with more severe disabilities.[7]

Another socio-spatial concept that is often used for the design of care sites and that has been introduced in care facilities under the Flemish policy of the 'socialization of care' is the idea of bringing the neighbourhood into the facility. One way of doing this is by promoting neighbourhood activities or integrating spaces for the neighbourhood into the design. Inclusion is thus measured on the basis of someone's participation in the neighbourhood, while for some people this leads to overstimulation and anxiety.

Monnikenheide shows that designing for inclusion involves more than the use of a number of socio-spatial concepts. The Monnikenheide site is located on the edge of the woods, separated from the village centre like a kind of enclave. Based on the conviction that care facilities should be integrated on a small scale in the village or town centre in order to promote social inclusion in a neighbourhood, Monnikenheide would therefore be founded on an undesirable spatial model for the inclusion of people with disabilities.

For Monnikenheide, the essence of working on inclusion lies elsewhere. What makes Monnikenheide truly inclusive is the constant drive to give residents the right to live in dignity and to claim their right to exist every day through a politics of presence. Initiators Wivina and Paul Demeester wanted to normalize interdependency and give the residents of Monnikenheide a family-oriented experience. To this end, they understood the importance of being anchored in a physical place. At the same time, they understood that the inhabitants of Zoersel would have to adapt to this, even if familiarizing them with 'the normality' of their guests was not a matter of course.[8]

In other words, Monnikenheide is imbued with a political awareness that the physical presence of people with disabilities is linked to their right to exist and that radical care is a political statement. Johanna Hedva formulated this political dimension of care powerfully: 'The most anti-capitalist protest is to care for an other and to care for yourself. To take on the historically feminized and therefore invisible practice of nursing, nurturing, caring. To take seriously each other's vulnerability and fragility and precarity, and to support it, honour it, empower it. To protect each other, to enact and practice a community of support. A radical kinship, an interdependent sociality, a politics of care.'[9]

TAKING PLACE: SPATIAL TOOLS

How do we translate this political view of care and inclusion into spatial terms? What can architects and planners learn from Monnikenheide?

Monnikenheide presents a spatial model for the radical inclusion of people in need of care that builds on the principles of a politics of presence. Where the concept of 'inclusion' still often assumes that 'we as a homogeneous society give permission to a marginalized community to occupy a place in our society', Monnikenheide answers: 'We as a marginalized community claim our place'.

Monnikenheide is designed on the basis of the feminist concept of 'taking place'. This spatial practice pays attention to mutual differences and 'otherness', not necessarily with the aim of being 'included' or 'represented', as in the definition of inclusion, but to take part in society directly from a differential position.[10] Wivina and Paul Demeester were aware of this importance from the start and drew inspiration from the concept of 'human territoriality': the importance of being able to occupy space and of being physically anchored in order to feel at home and develop oneself.[11] In her book *Belonging: A Culture of Place*, bell hooks also speaks about the important link between feeling at home and being physically anchored.[12]

In Monnikenheide, the politics of presence and the claim to 'take place' begin with the appropriation of a location in a green residential area that the average Flemish family dreams of living in. The site corresponds with the Flemish subdivision typology and nestles on the edge of the woods. However, the segregation of the location is not a metaphor for the exclusion of its residents. On the contrary, by claiming a space that the average Fleming would 'die for', it makes a political statement for the normalized living of people in need of care. With Huis aan de Kerk, Wivina and Paul Demeester wanted to literally build 'right under the church tower'. Based on the idea of a politics of presence, Monnikenheide normalizes the presence of people with a disability and their need for high-quality housing in the villagescape of Zoersel.[13]

Monnikenheide also shows that the right to quality architecture and having a beautiful home applies to everyone. A stable home environment and a quality home are crucial to everyone's well-being and self-development. Beautiful architecture makes people more beautiful, according to Wivina Demeester. The various pavilions and houses of Monnikenheide were designed by well-known Flemish architects: Huiswerk architecten, Vermeiren De

Coster Architecten, Jo Peeters, UR architects, 51N4E and FELT architecture & design. The notion of a politics of presence hence extends to the presence and visibility in Flemish architectural culture. 'We may be seen' creeps in like a soft credo based on a cultural appreciation of care architecture.

Monnikenheide was conceived on the basis of a vision of normalization, and this principle is also carried through in the architecture. Dirk Somers (for Huiswerk architecten) and Johan De Coster (at the time working as an intern for Mys-Bomans architecten) designed respectively Huis aan de Voorne and Huis aan de Kerk from the idea of the normal house in the street. However, designing from a vision of normality cannot be reduced to a focus on the banality or invisibility of architecture. Dirk Somers wanted to incorporate everyday characteristics of the environment in such a way that they were magnified and became special. Somers himself speaks of a 'transbanality'. The focus is not on the banal and invisible, but on normalizing housing for people in need of care. This means that residents can be proud of their homes and experience a radical homeliness. In this sense, the design and architectural style are of secondary importance. Sometimes the normality is expressed in a very commonplace, almost invisible architecture, such as Huis aan de Kerk, while at other times it entails a very visible architecture. For example, the latest house, Villa Kameleon by FELT, proudly adopts the detached villa typology of its closest neighbours.

What essentially distinguishes Monnikenheide is that one continually listens to the needs of the residents and explores how changing care needs can be given shape. Because some residents were limited in their independence at Monnikenheide, the decision was taken to build small-scale forms of sheltered housing closer to the village centre. This is how Huis aan de Voorne, Huis aan de Kerk and Villa Kameleon came about. The idea is that when the level of care needs to be increased, the resident can move to another accommodation within Monnikenheide. In this way, Monnikenheide provides a care continuum in which a variety of housing typologies and care support are utilized to meet a range of care needs and personal residential preferences. In essence, architects should prioritize the housing needs of residents, and should accommodate the (sometimes complex) care requirements. But today, the opposite often happens and the care issue is isolated, reducing people to their identity as care-dependent persons.

Monnikenheide shows how care architecture transcends the care sector. At a time when there is a crying need for new visions on co-existence, Monnikenheide shows how people can live together based on the principles of 'universal care'. This model places care at the centre of all scales of life – from the domestic sphere to our kinships, the state and the planet.[14]

CONCLUSION

Monnikenheide offers architects and clients a more politically conscious view of inclusion by basing architectural design on principles of universal care and a politics of presence. Wivina Demeester embodies the importance of a combined approach to care, architecture and politics. When she was given the opportunity to become a member of parliament and later a minister, she saw this as yet another step in trying to push through change. That same drive and political awareness marked the foundations of Monnikenheide and allowed the site to become an example of care architecture that deserves international attention. Designing beyond the illusion of inclusion requires designers and clients to take on a political role to eliminate structural inequalities and rewrite the norm. Politics does not start in the Chamber of Representatives, but in day-to-day design choices.

'Architecture is always political'
– Andrés Jaque

1. Jonathan Darling, 'Forced migration and the city: Irregularity, informality, and the politics of presence', *Progress in Human Geography*, 41(2) (2017), 178-198.
2. Antoine Printz, 'The EU's social and urban policies from the perspective of inclusion. History and usage of the concept', in *Designing Urban Inclusion*, eds. Mathieu Berger, Benoît Moritz, Louise Carlier, Marco Ranzato Brussels, Metrolab Series, #1 (2018), 183-193.
3. Printz, 'The EU's social and urban policies from the perspective of inclusion', 183-193.
4. Daniel Johnson, John Clarkson, Felicia Huppert, 'Capability measurement for Inclusive Design', *Journal of Engineering Design*, 21(2) (2010), 275-288.
5. Printz, 'The EU's social and urban policies from the perspective of inclusion'.
6. Virginie Cobigo, Hélène Ouellette-Kuntz, Rosemary Lysaght and Lynn Martin, 'Changing our conceptualization of social inclusion', *Stigma Research and Action*, 2(2), (2012), 75-84.
7. Cobigo, Ouellette-Kuntz, Lysaght and Martin, 'Changing our conceptualization of social inclusion'.
8. Wivina Demeester-De Meyer, Kris De Koninck, Johan Vermeeren, eds., Monnikenheide '40', (Zoersel: vzw Monnikenheide, 2014).
9. Johanna Hedva, 'Sick Woman Theory', *Mask Magazine*, January 2016.
10. Teresa Hoskyns and Doina Petrescu, 'Taking place and altering it', in *Altering Practices. Feminist Politics and Poetics of Space*, ed. Doina Petrescu (London: Routledge, 2007).
11. Cornelis Bakker C. and Marianne K. Bakker-Rabdau, *No trespassing! Explorations in human territoriality* (San Francisco: Chandler & Sharp Publishers, 1973).
12. bell hooks, *Belonging: a Culture of Place* (Abingdon: Routledge, 2009).
13. Darling, 'Forced migration and the city', 178-198.
14. The Care Collective, *The Care Manifesto: The Politics of Interdependence* (New York/London: Verso Books, 2020).

Ferraris map no. 107 'Santhoven', from the Atlas Ferraris, Cabinet Map of the Austrian Netherlands and the Principality of Liège, 1771-1778. © Royal Library KBR

Brussel, de 27 JUL 72

Nr MLV 14156

Mijnheer de Kabinetschef,

In antwoord op uw schrijven van 13 juni 1972, heb ik het genoegen U te kunnen mededelen dat de Genietroepen zullen belast worden met het uitvoeren van de aanleg van een baan in bergkiezel van ± 640 m2 en een parking van ± 100 m2 in MONNIKENHEIDE, Kort-verblijf-centrum voor mentaal gehandicapte kinderen te ZOERSEL.

Hoogstwaarschijnlijk zullen deze werken tegen 01 april 1973, vooropgestelde openingsdatum van het centrum, verwezenlijkt zijn voor zover de weersomstandigheden in 72/73 het zullen toelaten.

Tussen 4 januari en 14 maart 72 hebben de Genietroepen reeds belangrijke grondwerken te ZOERSEL uitgevoerd.

Het jaarprogramma der werken te realiseren door de Genie ten voordele van militaire en burgerorganismen - met filantropisch karakter - heeft een aanzienlijke vertraging opgelopen wegens de ongunstige weersomstandigheden van de eerste semester 1972.

De juiste aanvangsdatum, de uitvoeringsperiode en modaliteiten zullen ten gepaste tijde, zoals in het verleden, rechtstreeks geregeld worden tussen de Directie van het Centrum en de Commandant der Binnenlandse Verdedigingsstrijdkrachten - TERVUREN, verantwoordelijk voor het inzetten van de Genietroepen op het nationaal grondgebied.
De duur van de Genie-interventie werd op ± twee weken geschat.

Hoogachtend,

P. VANDEN BOEYNANTS
Minister

M. DUINSLAEGER
Kapitein ter Zee (D) MAB
Kabinetssecretaris

Aan de Heer G. HERTECANT
Kabinetschef
Ministerie van Volksgezondheid en van het Gezin
Administratief Centrum - Esplanadegebouw 5
1010 BRUSSEL

CARING FOR THE LANDSCAPE OF CARE
Gideon Boie and Vjera Sleutel

The landscape occupies a special place within the residential care programme at Monnikenheide. The woody environment is present everywhere as a generous setting for the accommodation of people with a mental disability. Intensive use of the landscape went hand in hand with rather extensive management of the woods. However, the new climate regime poses major challenges to the landscape of Monnikenheide, making it an increasingly urgent subject for discussion. In the margin of the design assignments for Monnikenbos and De Eiken, architect Regis Verplaetse (UR architects) elaborated a broad future vision for nature conservation.[1]

When Monnikenheide was launched, the rather coincidental choice of the woody estate, situated on the fault line between a typical Flemish subdivision and a nature reserve, proved to be a stroke of good luck.[2] When the non-profit organization Medische Inrichting en Openluchtwerken Sint-Godelieve (Medical Institution and Open-air Works Saint Godelieve) went out of business, the Zoerselhof Castle and surrounding grounds were sold in 1957 to a few directors who were involved, including Jozef Demeester, the father of Paul Demeester and father-in-law of Wivina Demeester. He later divided the property into four plots and donated one to the newly founded non-profit organization Monnikenheide, one to Wivina and Paul Demeester, and the other to his two daughters. The latter two plots were ultimately bought by the non-profit Monnikenheide.

The location says something about the ambition of the young couple to grant people with mental and physical disabilities the right to territoriality, a concept that Wivina Demeester derives from the environmental psychology of C.B. Bakker and M.K. Bakker-Rabdau.[3] Monnikenheide's low-stimulus, safe and open environment enables its residents to move about freely insofar as possible and to determine or shift boundaries. The village, and later the ever-growing surrounding subdivision, remains sufficiently close for contact to be maintained and mutual relations to be built up. In the spirit of the institutional criticism of the 1970s, Monnikenheide thus set the stage for a far-reaching normalization of care for people with a mental disability.

USE VALUES OF NATURE

At Monnikenheide, the deliberate use of nature for the purpose of care is paradoxically combined with the rather extensive management of that nature. The use of nature occurs spontaneously as part of everyday activities without there being a master plan for the green area or a specific design for the landscaping. The Monnikenheide estate has developed very organically over the years: with each new need for care, a suitable building location has been sought, often also strategically responding to different addresses. The 2012 vision document defines a number of key points related to good living, adapted living (only where necessary), sustainable building, optimum total ownership cost and continuous maintenance, but it barely touches on the outdoor area.[4]

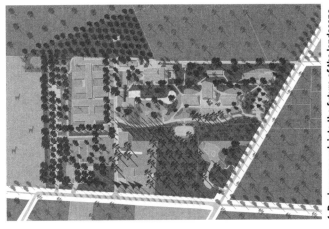

1. Design research into the future of the landscape of Monnikenheide by UR architects, 2022. © UR architects

The landscape interventions at Monnikenheide are punctual, like the gardening around the buildings. As early as the design by Bruno Boulanger in 1973 for the 'short-stay home' and the staff building, the plans show a garden around the building, with grass, shrubs, creepers, heath plants and other elements. The creator of the garden design was probably the architect himself. When the short-stay home was converted into the main building by architect Jo Peeters in 2003, the garden design was done by landscape architect Bart Jaeken. He planted clumps of elliptical shrubs around the building. Young trees accentuate the connection with the therapy pool and the laundry on the other side of the alley.

The jury report for the 2005 Bouwheer Prize, presented by the Flemish Government Architect, warned about the 'gardenization' of Monnikenheide as opposed to an 'actual landscaping integration'.[5] In response, landscape architect Paul Deroose, a member of the jury for the Flemish Government Architect, was commissioned for an environmental design for the conversion of Monnikenhuis into Zonnebloem (2010). The design consisted mainly of sowing Italian ryegrass, which after three years had the effect of restoring the woodland vegetation. At the time, the approach caused surprise among the staff, but the vegetation is still there today. The design also consisted of a terrace of bricks with a low hedge for relative privacy.

Nature also plays a role in the care programme of Monnikenheide as a free, virtually undetermined space. The educational footpath through the Doezelbos is exemplary in this respect. It has been open since 2009 to toddlers from schools in the area and connects to the regional bicycle network.[6] The residents of Monnikenheide act as *doezel* guides in the Doezel wood, after first taking an exam at Natuurpunt. The same woods are home to *Open kamer* (Open Room), a 2006 work by Richard Venlet that was created as part of the art integration during the renovation of the main building and serves as a stage for spontaneous use. The jury of the 2007 Bouwheer Prize praised the work as a 'building in the wrong place' inviting visitors to step off the beaten track.[7]

A CULTURAL-HISTORICAL ENVIRONMENT

The extensive management and spontaneous use of the landscape at Monnikenheide undoubtedly has great value in the residential care programme, but this should not disguise the fact that this environment is anything but wild nature. The genealogy of Monnikenheide taught architect Regis Verplaetse that throughout its history the landscape has been just as much a result of targeted interventions within a variety of plans. These cultural-historical values do not necessarily correspond to the current value of the

2., 3. Maintenance by residents of the former paddock, the horse stable is used today by the internal youth club. © Monnikenheide Archives

landscape within the care programme for people with a mental disability, but they do unconsciously play a major role. Verplaetse distinguishes three different structures in the morphology of Monnikenheide.

The first structure is the mixed oak-beech forest at the back of the estate, today among other things laid out as Doezelbos. From the thirteenth century onward, the land was part of St Bernard's Abbey in Hemiksem and was exploited as heathland, hence the name of the estate, Monnikenheide (Monk's Heath). From the eighteenth century onward, the open areas of heathland were systematically planted according to the 'trench and berm principle', drainage trenches being dug before trees were planted on the berms of residual earth. Traces of this element of forestry can be found on the remnants of the heathland in the surroundings of Monnikenheide, a landscape that today is partly managed by the Agency for Nature and Forests.

The landscape at the level of the main building has a quite different structure. It consists of a plantation of mature durmasts in an 8 m by 8 m grid. Today, this plantation acts as an alley within the care estate, but it was laid out in the interwar period as a view of the horizon at the Zoerselhof lawn. Zoerselhof was once intended as the abbot's residence for a Benedictine monastery that, in the end, was never built due to the French Revolution. Zoerselhof was the property of Baron Van de Put from 1912 to 1950, during which time it was transformed into a vast park with French and English garden landscaping and oaks forming an idyllic vista.

The third structure is the Norway spruce and fir plantation at the level of Huis aan 't Laar, built on an artificial hill in a clearing in the forest. The exact origin of the planting of these exotic tree species is uncertain, but recent height models suggest that these trees were also planted according to the trench and berm principle described above, possibly for private use. Finally, some of the trees in Monnikenheide were planted in the period after Monnikenheide was established, certainly in the initial phase, when a number of beeches were donated to the non-profit organization, and also later, during the environmental design carried out during the conversion of the main building.

THE LANDSCAPE IMPOSES ITSELF

In the current climate regime, however, the care landscape of Monnikenheide is under great pressure and demands urgent action. A few dry summers, for example, led to the rapid spread of the infamous bark beetle, which attacked the pine forest at Huis aan 't Laar to such an extent that its complete felling in 2021 was unavoidable. The sudden disappearance of the exotic trees was not only an attack on the identity of Monnikenheide, it also had repercussions on the architecture. After all, with the felling of the forest, there was no longer an open space in the forest, which was the guiding principle in the design of the Huis aan 't Laar in 2010.

Another example is the gradual dying out of the oak trees at the front of the estate. Although they were planted at the time as a horizon for the view from Zoerselhof, in the day-to-day operations of Monnikenheide they

4. Replanting of a native wood with a variety of species at Huis aan 't Laar in Spring 2022.
© UR architects

have come to function as alleys. Intensive use by the residents of the lawn between Seppenshuis, the main building and the old staff building (later known as Rode Roos) indirectly causes compaction of the soil. After all, the consistent clearing of fallen leaves removes nutrients from the soil, with disastrous consequences for the growth of the trees. There is now a regulation under which a zone must be demarcated around the oak trees within which the leaves must be left to rot and in which no one can play.

The changes show how the landscape of Monnikenheide silently tilted from a mere environment at the disposal of the care programme to something that itself requires special care. The evolution is a variation on the political analysis of Bruno Latour, who argued that today nature no longer functions as the constant backdrop against which the lives of residents are played out, but has stepped onto the stage and is claiming its place as an actor.[8] But the necessary care for the landscape chafes in the context of the welfare sector where there is an understandable tradition of investing the scarce resources into the clients, not in infrastructure works, let alone environmental design.

However, the new design challenge of the landscape will inevitably return to the agenda via annoying bark beetles or fragmentary discussions in the margins.[9] While the conversation began with the integration of the centuries-old oaks into the new De Eiken extension (2016), the focus naturally shifted to the management of the oaks on the lawn and then to the oaks in the parking lot behind the old staff building. In the same way, the construction of a bicycle shed at Doezelbos prompted discussions about depaving on the estate. Small interventions are thus key when it comes to thinking about the various dimensions of the ecosystem – nature, society and people – in all its reciprocal relations.[10]

THE CARE LANDSCAPE AS A DESIGN CHALLENGE

Other punctual interventions for nature conservation include the replanting of a native wood with a variety of species at Huis aan 't Laar, an experience garden on the former tennis court as compensation for the new car park at the Schaapskooi and safe islands for trees in the animal park. In the face of the new climate regime, the role of the architect is clearly changing from that of a service provider to that of a guardian who cares for the landscape and does so even without being asked.[11] After all, the conservation or restoration of nature does not fit so easily into well-defined project definitions with clear requirement programmes, well-defined responsibilities and fixed deadlines. Neither can nature conservation be reduced to a preliminary and definitive design.

Nature conservation therefore reaches a point where every decision has an impact on the entire organization of the care institution and thus threatens to thwart long-term decisions at different administrative levels. A decision in favour of nature can, just like that, jeopardize equally legitimate new building plans. Likewise, nature conservation may adversely affect care plans, because what is good for care is not always good for nature. For example, the

5. The new bicycle parking is equipped with a floating floor, which prevents compaction of the soil around the oaks, designed by UR architects, Spring 2023. © UR architects

recent addition of a few alpacas to the animal park is ideal for therapeutic purposes, but it is not easy to combine these animals with a woody biotope.

'Today we have to take extra care of nature if we want it to take care of us', said Regis Verplaetse after the felling of the pine forest at Huis aan 't Laar.[12] The design challenge of the care landscape is not easy to master because problems can arise today but solving them can take a long time. The slow realization is another reason why it would be beneficial to develop a shared vision of the landscape within the care centre, a vision that is supported by management, staff, residents, volunteers and the other parties involved. The only benefit of the painful felling of the coniferous wood is that it has made it clear to everyone at Monnikenheide that the landscape itself needs care if it is to provide care, as it has done spontaneously all these years.

1. This chapter is based on several interviews with initiator Wivina Demeester, technical director Kris De Koninck and architect Regis Verplaetse.
2. The history and ambitions of Monnikenheide are documented in: Wivina Demeester-De Meyer, Kris De Koninck and Johan Vermeeren, eds., *Monnikenheide '40'* (Zoersel: vzw Monnikenheide, 2014).
3. See C.B. Bakker and M.K. Bakker-Rabdau, *No Trespassing! Explorations in Human Territoriality* (San Francisco: Chandler & Sharp, 1973).
4. Kris De Koninck, *Samenvattende nota Strategie uitbouw en behoud van infrastructuur 2020*, approved by the Board of Directors on 20 June 2012.
5. Mat Steyvers, Pieternel Vermoortel and Edwin De Ceukelaire, *Prijs Bouwheer 2005 Juryverslag* (Brussels: Flemish Government Architect/Ministry of the Flemish Community, 2005).
6. Kristin Matthyssen, 'Gidsen met beperking zijn de échte natuurkrachten in Doezelbos van Monnikenheide', *Gazet van Antwerpen*, 5 October 2019. In 2018 the Doezelbos was awarded the Gouden Pagadder Prize by Beweging.net for the commitment of its volunteers.
7. *Open kamer* was nominated for the 2007 Bouwheer Prize of the Flemish Government Architect in the category 'Commissioned Art'. See: Sofie Vandelannoote, *Prijs Bouwheer 2007 Juryverslag* (Brussels: Flemish Government Architect, 2007). In an opinion piece, Wivina Demeester describes the function of the *Open kamer* as an indeterminate place: Wivina Demeester, 'Laat duizend kunsten bloeien', *De Standaard*, 13 March 2014.
8. Bruno Latour, *Down to Earth: Politics in the New Climatic Regime* (London: Polity, 2018), 43.
9. The 'return of the repressed' is a concept by which Slavoj Zizek indicates that things that are repressed inevitably surface in other places. See: Slavoj Zizek, *The Ticklish Subject* (London: Verso, 1999).
10. Félix Guattari, *The Three Ecologies* (London: Continuum, 2008 [1989]), 45.
11. Doina Petrescu speaks in this context of the architect-curator, indicating the new role that architects take on today as mediators of different desires. See: Doina Petrescu, 'Losing Control, Keeping Desire', in *Architecture and Participation*, Jones et al., eds. (London: Spon Press Taylor & Francis, 2005), 43–64.
12. Regis Verplaetse in a post on LinkedIn, 29 March 2022, last accessed 20 February 2023, https://www.linkedin.com/posts/regis-verplaetse-4755a733_healthcare-naturebasedsolutions-reforestation-activity-6914701422492053505-seVB/.

Image accompanying the article in the weekly magazine of the Algemeen Christelijke Werknemersverbond (Confederation of Christian Employees Union): M.P., 'Ten years of Monnikenheide', *Volksmacht* 21 (27 May, 1983), 12.

monnikenheide v.z.w.

kort-verblijf-centrum voor mentaal gehandicapte kinderen

secretariaat:
5, kasteeldreef   2153 zoersel

telefoon 03 - 721818

p.c. 673403 van kredietbank te westmalle
voor rek. nr 408 - 5010331 - 55

Vergelijking tussen de reële kostprijs en het vermoedelijk beschikbaar kapitaal.

Beschikbaar kapitaal		Reële kostprijs	
③ Boemerang	2.280.000.-		12.271.410.
④ Nationale Loterij	1.750.000.-	Kostprijs hoofdgebouw	12.028.785.-
① Staat	7.875.000.-	" personeelsgebouw	2.184.100.-
Eigen kapitaal op 11 maart 1972 (grond 1.milj.inbegrepen.)	3.700.000.-	Ereloon architect	450.000.-
			14.965.580.-
		BTW 14 %	2.086.742.-
② Provincie:20 % op de reële kostprijs	3.388.537.-		16.999.380.-
Provincie : 10.000.-/bed	350.000.-	Inrichting (Raming) BTW 18 %	2.000.000.- 360.000.-
Provincie : 20% vd.inrichtingskosten	436.000.-		19.362.888.-
		startgeld	1.500.000.-
totaal	19.779.537.-		20.803.688.-
		grond	1.000.000.-
		totaal	21.803.688.-

⑤ (Eigen) kapitaal . v.z.w.

VERSCHIL : 2.024.151.-

Demeester residence – Luc Van den Broeck, images from *Meubles et Décors* 884 (October 1973), 34-35.

DWELLINGS AT MONNIKENHEIDE
Gideon Boie and Vjera Sleutel

THE FIRST SETTLEMENT

The architectural history of Monnikenheide began when Wivina and Paul Demeester had a family home built adapted to their life style, and then immediately set to work on a short-term residence for the temporary accommodation of people with a mental disability. The subsequent building activity was characterized by a systematic expansion of housing facilities (for permanent and independent residence) and additional facilities (a staff building and workshop). These buildings form the stepping stones for later building projects and therefore recur in the overview. After all, buildings in Monnikenheide were not demolished but were given a new lease of life decades later after being renovated and expanded.

DEMEESTER RESIDENCE (1970)
The first building on Monnikenheide was the Demeester family's own home, also conceived as a directors' residence for the later care centre. Wivina and Paul Demeester called on architect Luc Van den Broeck, a family friend. The house is located on the public road, but is explicitly oriented towards the estate behind it. The carport is located on the front side wall along a forest road that would later develop into Monnikenheide's central alley. On the garden side, the house opens up to the wooded surroundings. Separated from the house, garden walls stand at half height, screening off the windows of the children's rooms and playroom on the one hand, and the dining area and back kitchen on the other. The projecting roof provides a covered outdoor area.

All the rooms in the house are on one level. The open kitchen flows into the large living area and playroom. The fireplace is a central element in the large, uncluttered space. A supporting structure of laminated beams allows the flat roof to be completely detached from the walls below. The cantilevered roof marks out the communal and intimate parts of the house. Because the private house serves as office space for the management of the care centre, the night area was soon redistributed. In 1976 the house was extended with an office, library and extra bedroom. As a result of this extension, the new entrance to the house was placed next to the carport.

SHORT-STAY HOME (1973)
The first construction project consisted of a 'short-stay home', as it was called on the building plans, designed by architect Bruno Boulanger. The preliminary design dates from 1969 and was produced by architect Juan Meyers of nv Seghers-Dinaco. The idea of a short-stay home responded to the need to temporarily relieve families of their burden in the event of a hospital admission or during a busy period or holidays, and thus to reinforce the capacity of the surroundings. The scale of the infrastructure is in keeping with the principle of the community as surrogate family. The short-stay home offers accommodation to five groups of seven children, up to age 21, for a period of minimum fourteen days and maximum three months. The Danilith construction system and the efforts of many volunteers made it possible to open the doors of the short-stay home after only eight months of work.

The short-stay home consists of four identical pavilions with a single storey. They are located at right angles to the central alley, so that the frontage is characterized by short, front façades. The two outer pavilions house two groups, with boys and girls strictly separated. Each group has a living room, dining area and kitchen combined with a bathroom and two communal bedrooms. The intermediate pavilions house the reception, kitchen, offices, therapy rooms, sandpit and therapy pool. Two large play areas connect the two outer pavilions with the groups and the central pavilions with central services, making circulation space unnecessary in these places.

STAFF BUILDING (1973)
A staff building was erected at the front of the estate and stands at right angles to the short-stay home. Bruno Boulanger's design is identical to the short-stay home. The short-stay home was conceived as a community along the lines of L'Arche, an initiative by Jean Vanier for integrated housing for disabled people in France, but at Monnikenheide the staff do not live among the residents. The starting point was that the care task was already heavy enough for the staff, who in the initial period often consisted of volunteers and were employed for a fixed period. The staff building made it possible to separate the staff's free time from the care work.

The building consists of a short corridor with five bedrooms on either side and communal bathroom facilities. The head of the building contains a shared living area with a kitchen. The entrance faces the Demeester residence on the other side of the open lawn. The construction makes it possible for the staff building to function later with striking ease as a care residence for elderly people with high care requirements under the name of De Wei (The Meadow). As part of the renovation and expansion of the short-stay home in 2003, a connection was made with the staff building via a corridor with glass façades. The staff building was then put into use for active residents under the name Rode Roos (Red Rose).

MONNIKENBOS (1980)
The demand grew for permanent accommodation for people with a mental disability in order to relieve parents who were getting too old or for whom the care task was too heavy. A separate non-profit organization, Monnikenbos, was set up to build an 'occupational home for mentally disabled adults' on a plot adjoining Monnikenheide. The new residence was given its own address on the Schaapskooi forest lane, at the back of the estate, to emphasize the difference between the two organizations. Monnikenbos was

designed by architect Luc Van den Broeck and consists of a complex of three care homes for six to seven people, linked by a multipurpose hall for daytime activities.

The buildings feature dark-brown brick and an oversized gable roof with grey slates. The raised ridge and large roof windows let zenithal northern light penetrate into the heart of the multipurpose space. The interior was given a rough finish with high-speed building bricks and wooden trusses. In the dwellings, veranda-like corner windows and large sliding doors establish a relation with the green surroundings. Large spaces were divided into corners, offering security to the heterogeneous group of residents. The focal point of each dwelling is the living room with an open kitchen. The sitting area with indoor plants, the carpet with decorative motif, the frivolous lampshade and the dining room with an open bookcase create a homely atmosphere.

MONNIKENHUIS (1980)

It is during the construction of Monnikenbos that the idea grew for Monnikenhuis, an experimental project for independent living that benefited from European subsidies. The building provides accommodation for four people (two men and two women) who live independently with limited supervision. The concept of independent living for people with a mental disability was unique at the time and started for a trial period of eight months under the supervision of a psychologist. Despite considerable doubt about the feasibility (even within the organization itself), the residents of Monnikenhuis were given a high degree of independence and were encouraged to make their own choices about how to spend their time.

Monnikenhuis was also designed by architect Luc Van den Broeck in the same style as Monnikenbos, but now as an independent residence. The somewhat secluded location of Monnikenhuis emphasizes its disconnection from the day-to-day activities of the care centre. The residents had their own entrance, house number and letter box. However, the protection of the 'mother hen' Monnikenbos was never far away. Monnikenbos eventually acquired a structural effect and laid the foundations for the later development of Huis aan de Voorne (The House at the River Voorne), where independent living is incorporated into the fabric of the village. The initiative also served as an early forerunner of the new regulations on sheltered housing for people with a mental disability.

WERKHUIS (1985)

The construction of Werkhuis (Workshop) made it possible to separate the living and working environment for the permanent residents of Monnikenheide. Based on the principle of normalization, a traditional workweek was arranged for the residents, despite the official label of incapacity to work. Residents worked during the day, went home in the evening and enjoyed free time at the weekend. At first, the central room in Monnikenbos was used for this purpose, but it soon proved to be too small. As the management had no intention of setting up new building projects, the staff took the initiative.

The workshop was designed by architect Mark Depreeuw, active in the later non-profit Flemish Institute for Bio-Environmental Building and Living (VIBE). The building was constructed by the non-profit organization Bouworde, led by brother Georges. Today, the workshop provides various craft ateliers, such as a bakery, farm work, woodworking and a diet kitchen. The stepped structure, the windows with bevelled corners and the jagged roof shape suggest a slightly anthroposophical aesthetic. The atmosphere within the workshop was determined by the use of high-speed building bricks and a brick floor. The large building height contrasts with the residential quarters in the surrounding area. The large dormers give the house an almost sacral impression, earning the workshop the nickname 'The Cathedral'.

Short-Stay Home – Bruno Boulanger © Monnikenheide Archives

Monnikenbos – Luc Van den Broeck © Monnikenheide Archives

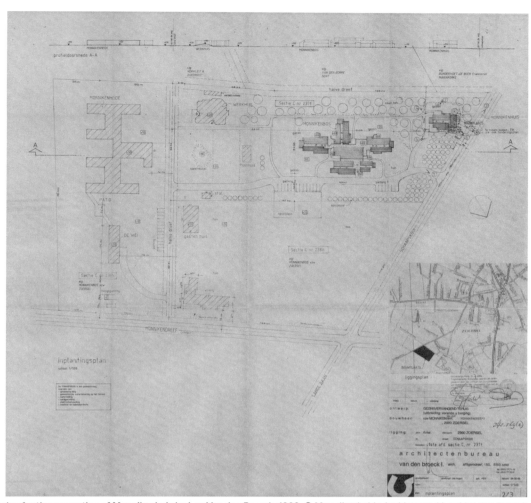

Situation plan for the renovation of Monnikenhuis by Luc Van den Broeck, 1998. © Monnikenheide Archives and Luc Van den Broeck

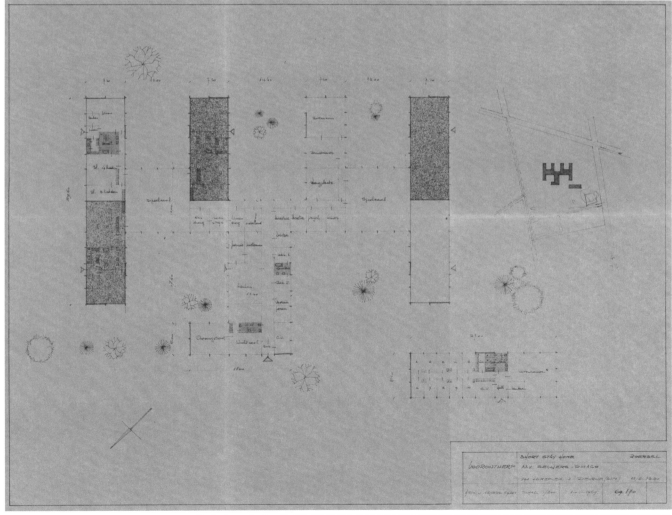

Preliminary design for the short-stay home by Juan Meyers, 1969. © Monnikenheide Archives and Juan Meyers

A HOUSE OF CULTURE ON THE CARE CAMPUS

PROJECT NAME
Seppenshuis
DESIGNER
bOb Van Reeth
– ArchitectenWerkGroep
CLIENT
Rachel Jacobs nv
LOCATION
Monnikendreef 7, 2980 Zoersel
DESIGN
1994
DELIVERED
1997
STUDY OFFICE
G. Derveaux nv
STUDY OFFICE TECHNOLOGIES
Studiebureel Minne bvba
MAIN CONTRACTOR
Van Roey nv
SURFACE AREA
439 m²
VOLUME
1,626 m³
TOTAL BUILDING COST
452,645 euro
TOTAL BUILDING COST PER M²
1,031 euro
PHOTOGRAPHY
Wim Van Nueten, except p. 82: Reiner Lautwein

Seppenshuis (House of Seppe) is a stately building with a bright-red brick façade and large windows under its roof. It stands on the central alley of Monnikenheide. The iconic design by bOb Van Reeth (ArchitectenWerkGroep) includes a study, library, conference and exhibition hall, and guest accommodation. It was built in 1997 on the private initiative of Wivina and Paul Demeester and the name Seppe honours Jozef, Paul's father, who had donated the properties to the family and the non-profit Monnikenheide. Although Seppenshuis does not have a direct care function, its cultural activities nevertheless play a special role within the care centre. In the pursuit of inclusion for people with a mental disability, it is equally important to normalize the significance of a care centre and open it up to a different public.

The double-height, multifunctional hall is the heart of Seppenshuis. It is where visitors are received. The various functions are arranged in an L-shape around the large hall. The entrance, cloakroom and sanitary facilities are located in the length of the building and seem to disappear into wall units fitted with acoustic oak panels. Above this wall is a mezzanine made of laminated wood that serves as a library and study area. The kitchen, stairwell and service entrance are on the short side. The top floor is home to three guest rooms, visually separated from the rest of the building.

The central space radiates an almost sacral character due to the striking proportions and even distribution of daylight. Seppenshuis was designed on the basis of the modular dimension of 2.70 m. This dimension lends rhythm to all the spaces, in height, width and depth. The hall's high ceiling consists of sheets of sandblasted glass and filters the daylight that enters through the higher windows. The shadows of the supporting structure at the back with so-called spiders make up a whimsical decorative element in the sober design. A large vertical window opening at the end of the hall reflects the sunlight falling on the pond, designed by landscape architect Bart Jaeken. A narrow double door provides direct access to the garden.

The narrow high door in the hall is covered on the outside with facing brick and thus blends into the façade. The playful choice of materials is also reflected in the interior design. The floor of the main hall is covered with oak parquet, and the floor of the entrance and the serving areas is of polished concrete. The hardened glass in the ceiling recurs as a balustrade on the mezzanine, a protection on the staircase and a dividing wall in the guest rooms. The large hall is divided by a ceiling-high curtain on rails that circle the entire space.

Seppenshuis is strategically located on the border of the private property of Wivina and Paul Demeester. The building thus subtly marks a boundary between the private house and the care centre, while also building numerous bridges. Seppenshuis therefore has several entrances. The main entrance is in the end wall and can be reached along a path that starts at the villa of the Demeester family, where the car park used to be. The service entrance in the longitudinal façade gives onto the central alley and offers easy access from the main building, where the path now runs along De Eiken (The Oak Trees) to the new car park. Lastly, the hidden, brick-covered door opens directly onto the private garden and uses the sculpture garden as an extension of Seppenshuis.

A pond girdles the building and seems to emphasize the outline of Seppenshuis from the collective and private property. The outline is reinforced by a zinc plinth that has been set back to make the building float slightly above its surroundings. The high, blind brick façade also seems to emphatically withdraw from the busy daily routine in the care centre and thus to create space for other activities. The art exhibitions, concerts and conferences are important as intermediary programmes that welcome outsiders to Monnikenheide, which is ultimately part of the drive towards inclusion. In this perspective, the guest rooms also offer the possibility of spending longer periods of time on the estate.

Seppenshuis also played a role in the development of Monnikenheide as a knowledge centre. Since the start in 1970, Wivina and Paul Demeester have nurtured the ambition to collect innovative knowledge and make it available as a common good. To this end, they undertook internships abroad to learn about other forms of organization for people with a mental disability. This quest was translated in the experimental building projects at Monnikenheide. Later, international collaborations were set up with Monnikenheide as an example. In this dynamic, Seppenshuis acted as the physical place for knowledge exchange on the inclusion of people with a disability.

Level 0
Level 1, Level 2

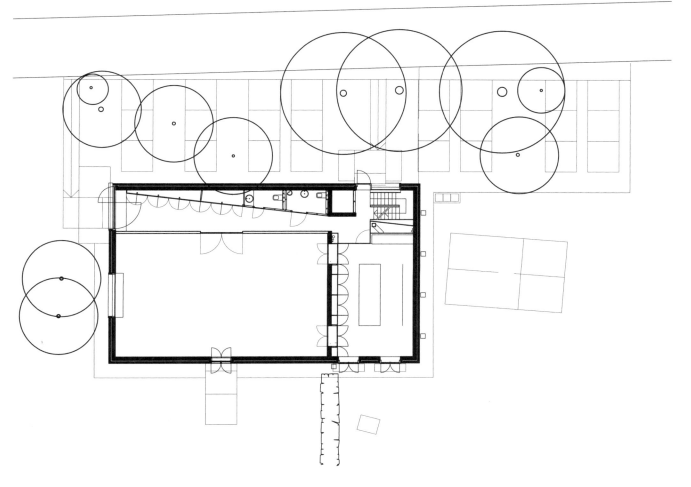

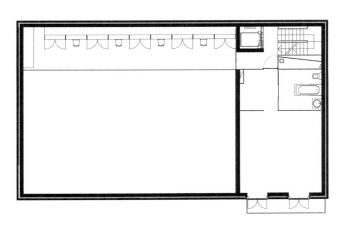

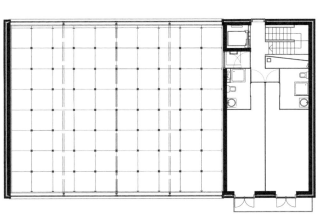

West Elevation, East Elevation

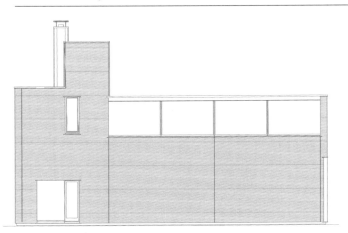

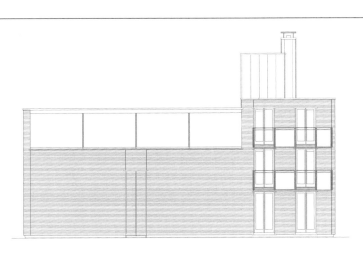

Seppenshuis · bOb Van Reeth – ArchitectenWerkGroep

PROJECT NAME
　Annexe to Demeester residence
DESIGNER
　Maarten Van Severen
EXECUTIVE ARCHITECT
　Erik Roels
CLIENT
　Wivina and Paul Demeester-De Meyer
LOCATION
　Monnikendreef 5, 2980 Zoersel
DESIGN
　2000
SURFACE
　140 m²
TOTAL BUILDING COST
　90,000 euro, incl. bookcase
BUILDING COST PER M²
　643 euro
COST OF FURNITURE
　7,934 euro
PHOTOGRAPHY
　Dries Luyten

A TOTAL DESIGN FOR THE WORKSPACE

The many meetings inherent to the position of director and later also minister proved difficult to combine with family life in a house with an open floor plan. As early as 1976, the house was extended with an annexe designed by Luc Van den Broeck, who had designed the house in 1970. The extension created space for an office for Wivina Demeester and for a private studio for her son Steven, who has Down syndrome. In 2000 Maarten Van Severen was commissioned to furnish Wivina Demeester's office. From the first meeting, the assignment grew into a complete renovation of the annexe, with a precise scenography for the workspace. Architect Erik Roels carried out the design.

The office space was fitted with furniture designed by Maarten Van Severen. The central piece is a T88A table with a worktop in roughly polished aluminium, manufactured by Lensvelt (1988). The large table virtually fills the office space. The roughly polished aluminium top reflects the books open on the table as well as the stationery. The .04 office chair was combined with two chairs from the .03 series for guests. Both chairs were designed for the furniture manufacturer Vitra in 2000 and 1998, respectively. Zenithal light falls on the desk through a pyramidal glass dormer seamlessly integrated into the ceiling.

A large bookcase stands at the back of the desk. Made of sheets of glass glued together invisibly, the bookcase fills the entire wall from the entrance to the storage. The completely transparent vertical and horizontal glass panels allow the rows of books to flow through as an unending pattern of colour and form. Built into the ceiling, the lighting runs the entire length of the bookcase, a variation on Maarten Van Severen's bookcase design for the Maison à Bordeaux by Rem Koolhaas (OMA) in Floirac, where semi-translucent glass panels were used.

The lounge is home to two LCP00 chairs, two low plastic lounge chairs combined with a baroque sofa. The LCP00 consists of a smoothly folded surface of transparent plastic without armrests or legs. It was produced by the Kartell furniture manufacturer in 2000. The structure is not completely closed, so that you feel a slight spring when you sit down. From the low ergonomic sculpture, you can look out on the surroundings of Monnikenheide as you would a sublime painting with tall pine trees and lush greenery. Because the window has no visible frame, the entire lounge functions as a frame for the outdoors, conceived from the centrally positioned office chair.

The meeting room is a rather closed room, with glass bookcases arranged on the two side walls. Again, the meeting room is completely occupied by a large T88A table and chairs from the .03 series. A large, floor-to-ceiling corner window provides an oblique line of sight straight across the room onto Seppenshuis and the estate's central alley. The window opening has a concealed frame in the ceiling and floor. The light-grey, seamless cast floor connects the various rooms and, at the express request of the client, was inspired by the floor in the kitchen of Maison à Bordeaux.

A doorway gives direct access from the hallway to the lounge that doubles as a reception area. A glass sliding wall screens off the office space from the reception room. When closed, the translucent glass reveals nothing but the shadows of what is going on behind it. The glass sliding wall, which disappears into the walls on the side of the library/meeting room, closes off the front door and integrates the entrance into the office space. Rails are integrated in the ceiling. Two sliding walls can close off the lounge on the side of the front door and the meeting room. The sliding walls are embedded in the surface of the walls. Heating has also been integrated in the floor in order to perfectly frame the view of the front garden.

During the renovation, the volume of the extension was corrected to a perfect square. The existing window openings at breast height were replaced with floor-to-ceiling windows. The office, lounge and meeting room were fitted into the square. Steven Demeester's bedroom and walk-in wardrobe are also located in the extension but were kept almost intact at the client's request. The new front door to the workspace, a striking reflective yellow glass panel, will function de facto as the entrance to the entire house, with the extension acting as a mediating in-between space. However, the unobtrusive path running along the carport and leading to the original front door was retained.

The materiality of the extension departs from that of the existing house. The gray bevelled roof edge contrasts sharply with the dark-wood roof edge of the existing house but lies perfectly in the same horizontal line. Parts of the dark brick façade of the existing house remain visible, while other parts of the façade were covered with sheets of glass. The alternately transparent and coloured reflective glass creates striking compositions. The colour in the glass is not a finishing layer but lies behind the glass and thus appears as an intrinsic part of the building. All the different colours of glass reflect the natural surroundings and thus give the workspace a hushed atmosphere.

PROJECT NAME
Huis aan de Voorne
DESIGNER
Huiswerk architecten
CLIENT
Monnikenheide vzw
LOCATION
Voorne 1, 2980 Zoersel
DESIGN
2000
DELIVERY
2003
STUDY OFFICE STABILITY
Newton bvba
MAIN CONTRACTOR
Bouwonderneming Dillen bvba
SURFACE
365 m²
VOLUME
1,130 m³
TOTAL BUILDING COST PER M²
1,300 euro, excl. VAT
PHOTOGRAPHY
Niels Donckers, except p. 94: Karin Borghouts

THE VILLAGE AS CARE ENVIRONMENT

Just outside the village centre of Zoersel stands a house in the ribbon development along the river Voorne. It is an everyday scene in urbanized Flanders, except that the detached house stands out somewhat excessively, in line with the sometimes gaudy villas further on. Huis aan de Voorne (The House at the River Voorne) comprises eight individual studios. People with mental and physical disabilities live there independently. The house was built in 2003 as part of Monnikenheide and is considered one of the early initiatives for sheltered accommodation. The design by Dirk Somers (then active in Huiswerk architecten, today in Bovenbouw Architectuur) deserves an iconic place in care architecture in Flanders, and this for several reasons.

The detached house is a fairly literal translation of the desire to create an inclusive and normalized living environment, although one that is adapted to the needs and desires of the residents. The building envelope creates the primitive image – the architect speaks of a 'childlike literalness' – of a house with a roof and front door. The front door opens directly onto the hall and the living area. At the same time, this central living area is an atrium that extends over the three storeys and looks out onto the ascending corridor around which the rooms are arranged. The corridor thus disappears as a circulation space and presents itself as a rising, stately space from which one can oversee the entire building.

During the design phase, the future residents emphasized their desire for individuality and privacy. The design therefore emphasizes the independence of the residents rather than a sense of community. The central living space is rather minimal and functions simultaneously as a sitting room, dining room and kitchen. It is a communal space that serves as a transition between the private studios of the residents. The studios are spacious rooms with their own sitting area, sanitary corner and kitchenette. Remarkably, the door to the studios is conceived as a front door. The architect recalls that, when he asked the question 'Is there anything else we haven't thought of?', he received the witty reply: 'Yes, a woman.'

The care home, part of Monnikenheide, was the first facility to be built outside the protected environment of the woods, a little further down the side street. The location of Monnikenheide on the edge of the forest and the subdivision was good for accommodating people with mental and physical disabilities in an open environment. However, this restricted the independence of some residents. In response, a house on the Voorne was purchased for the independent accommodation of three residents. The location on the village street made it easier to use the social facilities in the village (bakery, grocery shop, bus stop, etc.).

Technical director Kris De Koninck remembers how, at the time, he had to fight the cliché that the residents would fail to feed or wash themselves in the morning – as if no support were available from Monnikenheide. Nevertheless, the inclusion proved to be a success and plans were soon made to increase the housing capacity and quality. Due to the limited typology of the existing home, the decision was made to demolish and build anew, with the added advantage that the existing house at the back of the plot could remain operational during the construction of the new house in the front garden. This is also the reason why the new building is now close to the street and the back garden has remained as open as possible.

The design of Huis aan de Voorne engages in a rhetorical game with conventions and commonplaces of the village environment. For example, the large roof made it possible to build a third storey in a context where this is not allowed in principle – a solution that is also visible in the large *fermettes* further on. The red bricks emphatically show that this is a house, not a care institution – the architect explicitly rejected the slick design that is usually supposed to mask hospital standards for ergonomics, hygiene and the like.

The architect calls the design style 'hysterically contextual', a term he adopted from his then internship supervisor and current Flemish Government Architect, Erik Wieërs. It means that the house shamelessly incorporates everyday characteristics of the environment and magnifies them in such a way as to make them special. The large red brick façade is an interpretation of the houses in the village. The scale refers more to the villas in the subdivision of the forest. The tiled floor with a Vichy pattern is a nod to the tablecloth in the Flemish rear kitchen. The architect calls the design of Huis aan de Voorne a case of 'transbanality': a range of banal features that are characteristic of a domestic atmosphere are translated into a care context.

Strikingly, the most important reference project was the entrance building of the Hoge Rielen holiday park. 'Both projects marinated at the same time', says the architect with a wink. Perhaps that is where the uniqueness of Huis aan de Voorne lies: the house not only ensures the inclusion of people with a physical and mental disability in the village environment, it also deviates from the typical *sickly* design of hospitals and shelters.

Level 0, Level 1
Level 2, Level 3

0 2m

 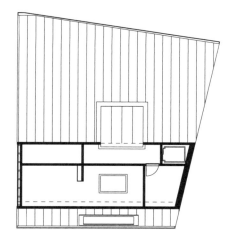

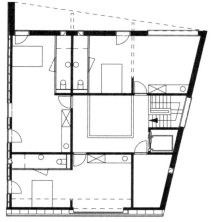

North Elevation, Section

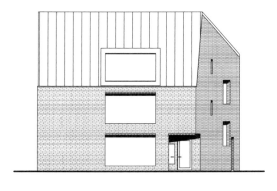 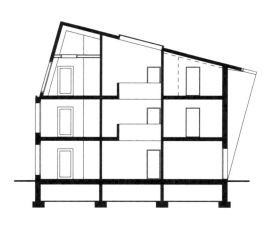

Situation Plan

0 10m

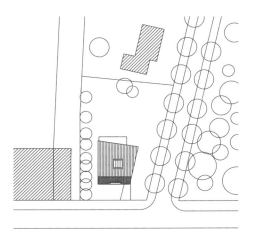

Huis aan de Voorne   95   Huiswerk architecten   4

PROJECT NAME
: Main building, therapy pool and laundry
DESIGNER
: Architectuurgroep Jo Peeters
CLIENT
: Monnikenheide vzw
LOCATION
: Monnikendreef 3, 2980 Zoersel
DESIGN
: 2001
DELIVERY
: 2003
MAIN CONTRACTOR
: Van Roey nv
STUDY OFFICE STABILITY
: Newton bvba
STUDY OFFICE TECHNOLOGIES
: IRS Studiebureau bvba
SURFACE
: 3,140 m²
TOTAL BUILDING COST
: 3,418,008 euro
TOTAL BUILDING COST PER M²
: 1,088 euro
PHOTOGRAPHY
: Dries Luyten

A LIVELY COMPLEX ON THE ALLEY

The central alley at Monnikenheide is dominated by several rectilinear volumes with an additional superstructure. On the other side of the alley are two open glass pavilions with a therapy pool and laundry. Large, floor-to-ceiling windows provide a link between life in the buildings and the green surroundings. A resident waves to the gardener from his seat. Small gardens have been laid out between the repeated buildings where other residents chat about the lady at work in the laundry. The administration is housed in the raised floor, and once again the glass façade and glass partitions provide great transparency.

The complex is a 2003 conversion and extension by Architectuurgroep Jo Peeters of the first group of buildings on the site, initially developed as a 'short-stay home' in 1973. The four original volumes, built using the Danilith construction system, were converted into care homes and extended at their extremities. In the same rhythm, one house was added in an aesthetic that ties in closely with the previous brick architecture. With a subtle difference in colour in the brickwork, the architect reveals where the boundary lies between existing and added construction. The openness to the surroundings was emphasized by the execution of the top of the houses with glass façades that extend above the roof and are even emphasized with an LED strip.

The different volumes were conceived as separate homes with a glass living room overlooking the central alley (the architect called this space 'the cockpit'). Because the architect had no experience in the care sector, design choices were motivated by a perception of space that applies equally to housing or catering. A wall creates privacy for the dining room, kitchen and Snoezelen sensory therapy room. The open kitchen can be closed off with a sliding wall. The bedrooms were converted into individual rooms, accessible via a joinery wall that also functions as a storage space. The bedroom wall with a window was painted black to emphasize the view.

The multipurpose rooms between the original pavilions were demolished and replaced by a long corridor that strings the five volumes together. The therapy pool and the laundry were moved to the other side of the alley, in separate pavilions, in order to heighten the dynamism around the alley. After much discussion, the corridor was retained for the sake of practical contact and support between the care homes, which provide accommodation for residents in need of care. The corridor was provided with glass façades, however, so that there is a generous view of the individual pavilions and the green surroundings. The corridor's width means the circulation area also doubles as a multipurpose activity area. The corridor was extended to the old staff building, which now functions as the Rode Roos (Red Rose) department.

The front of the middle pavilion projects forward explicitly and marks the central reception area with a steel canopy. The entrance pavilion gives onto the kitchen, dining room and multipurpose room in the corridor. It also provides access to the offices in the structure. A steel construction with cross joints on the roof was necessary in order to build on the light, system-based construction from the 1970s. The execution in glass and steel not only contrasts with the brick houses, it also creates a very transparent work environment. The individual worktables and conference rooms are separated by glass partitions and half-height cabinets. This allows an exchange between different sections of staff.

The transition between the indoor area and the green surroundings is most striking in the therapy pool, on the other side of the central alley. The swimming pool flows optically into the adjoining pond. The tall trees are reflected in the glass and the sunlight shines on the water. As a result, the ducks seem to swim side by side with the residents inside. The glass façades and concrete façade panels ensure a visual connection between the therapy pool and the laundry on the other side of the footpath. The stately housing and central position of the laundry is remarkable for a function that is usually accommodated in dark back rooms. This raises the status of the laundry and allows it to develop into a place for living and learning.

Unravelling the programme into four different identities – housing, administration, therapy pool and laundry – breaks with the original layout. In the former situation, the four volumes on either side contained the short-stay groups, with a strict separation between boys and girls. The volumes in-between contained all the other functional areas. Over the years, several elements were added, so that the building grew into a veritable maze of corridors and doors. The new design has created a legibility that is often lacking in care institutions. The lively complex thus forms the foundation that allows the central alley to develop into a village street, where you meet people right and left.

Main building   98   Architectuurgroep Jo Peeters

Level 1 (offices), East Elevation

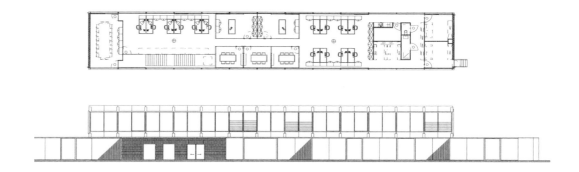

Level 0, Therapy Pool and Laundry

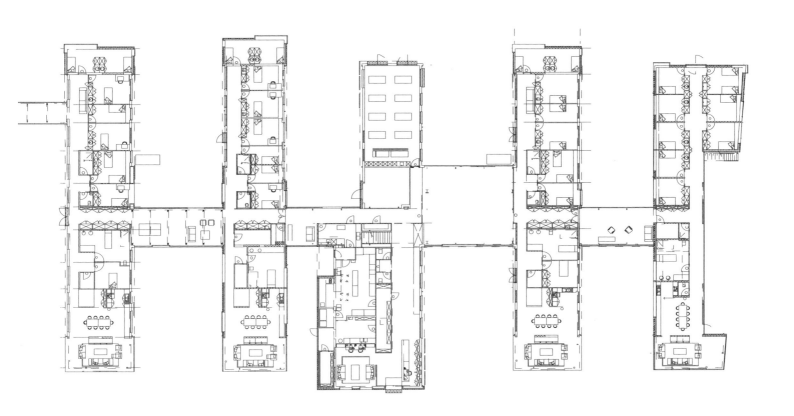

Main building — Architectuurgroep Jo Peeters

PROJECT NAME
Huis aan de Kerk
DESIGNER
Vermeiren De Coster Architecten
CLIENT
Monnikenheide vzw
LOCATION
Kerkstraat 20, 2980 Zoersel
DESIGN
February 2003
DELIVERY
November 2004
STUDY OFFICE STABILITY
Bart Velleman
MAIN CONTRACTOR
Noordbouw nv
SURFACE
416 m²
VOLUME
1,330 m³
TOTAL BUILDING COST
428,000 euro
TOTAL BUILDING COST PER M²
1,029 euro
PHOTOGRAPHY
Niels Donckers

DESIGNING THE NORMALIZATION OF CARE

Right under the church tower in Zoersel stands a vast residence. It is home to seven studios for people with a mental and physical disability who usually work during the day. Huis aan de Kerk (The House at the Church) was built in 2004 as the successor to Huis aan de Voorne (The House at the River Voorne). It goes one step further in the inclusion of disabled people in the social fabric. The design by Johan De Coster (then as a trainee at Mys-Bomans architecten, today at Vermeiren De Coster Architecten) aims to give residents far-reaching independence. The modest design and the choice of location are paradoxically the core of a political statement about normalized living for residents in need of care.

The design explicitly seeks to create a homely atmosphere. The front door gives access directly to the hall and the living room, which looks like the living room of any family home. Even the interior decoration and furniture hardly betray the fact that living here is somehow different. In a generous double-height room, the staircase flows into the living room, dining room and open kitchen. A large window draws the dining area as far as possible into the deep garden and fills the house with light. To enhance the feeling of homeliness, the common areas were finished with a parquet floor.

Seven studios are arranged around the central hall. As a result, the circulation space is minimal. Each studio has its own sanitary facilities and a kitchenette. Because the building is intended for very independent residents, the sense of homeliness could be maximized. There is no separate room for care staff and no compromises were made on the pretext of flexibility. There is even no lift. The idea is that, if care needs to be scaled up, the residents can be moved to another accommodation within Monnikenheide. Nor have fire safety standards been heightened. The communal areas flow into each other, all the way to the stairs. The simple solution was to treat every studio door as a fire door.

The spatial setting marks a break with the past at Monnikenheide. The care home lies outside the protected environment of the woods, following the good example of Huis aan de Voorne. In the form of a terraced house, Huis aan de Kerk blends into the village fabric. The building adjoins the neighbouring one- or two-storey houses with gabled roof and the obligatory dormer windows. The house looks out on a primary school and the church. It replaces two existing dwellings and fills this space with a programme of seven studios (which appeared to be the maximum feasible). The integration of the care home into the village is emphasized by the smooth, bright-red bricks and roof tiles.

The extensive programme seeks out the limits of the small building envelope. The façade is set back at the terrace level on the first floor, at the height of the neighbours' rain gutter. As such, it connects with what the architect calls the 'grain of the context'. The terrace also allows daylight to penetrate deep into the house. The house occupies all of the permitted building depth. As a result, the rear façade is not parallel to the front façade and the roof at the rear has a strikingly sloping connection. The free side wall is slanted at ground level to let cars and bicycles into the garden. The overhang on the side wall shows how the building envelope was used to maximum effect.

The basic idea was to think through all aspects of the homeliness, the architect explains. The homely organization and homely materials ensure that everything is done 'literally as it would be for any other home'. The typical clinical design of care centres is therefore nowhere to be seen, and medical standardization is no longer perceptible in the materials. The fact that the architect had no experience whatsoever in the field of care is a good thing in this respect. It seems to be a case of invisible care avant la lettre, the architecture enabling the residents to fully participate in village life. Assistance with cooking does not detract from the fact that, like the other villagers, the residents have to get up early for work before they can sink down into their lazy chairs in the evening.

Paradoxically enough, the invisible, almost trivial homeliness is a major statement. 'It was a statement by Wivina Demeester to make integrated living possible for people with a mental disability, right in the middle of the village, literally under the church tower,' says the architect. The private funds meant that the standards of the Flemish Infrastructure Fund for Person-related Matters (VIPA) did not apply. Furthermore, the safety regulations were brought into line with the concept in a creative way. Complaints about the care home being built too close to the church and about the less than refined design were beside the point. Almost twenty years after it was opened, Wivina Demeester remains resolute: 'A discussion about style misses the point that this home does a fine job of pressing home normality.'

Level 0, Level 1
Level 2

0　2m

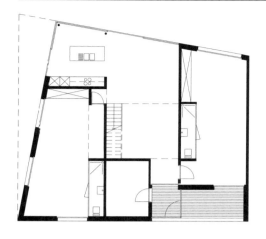
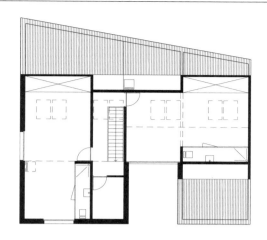

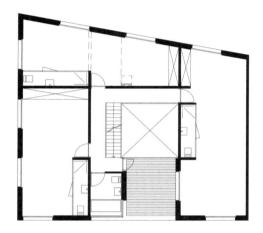

Section, North Elevation

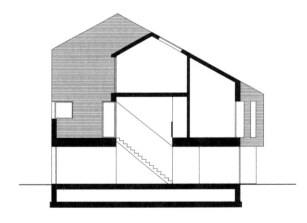
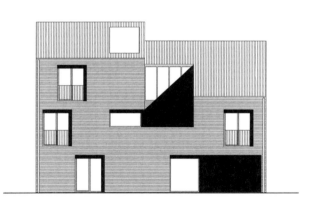

Situation Plan

0　20m

Huis aan de Kerk　　　105　　　Vermeiren De Coster Architecten

PROJECT NAME
Open kamer
DESIGNER
Richard Venlet
CLIENT
Monnikenheide vzw
LOCATION
Doezelbos, Monnikenheide
DELIVERY
2006
PHOTOGRAPHY
Richard Venlet

A ROOM IN THE WOODS

A reflecting door gleams in the forest at the edge of the care centre. The door stands freely on a concrete slab that seems to float above the ground. The installation defines an idiosyncratic space without walls or roof. Welcome to *Open kamer* (Open Room), a work of art commissioned by Monnikenheide and conceived by Richard Venlet in 2006. The piece came about as an integrated work of art during the renovation of the main building after 1 per cent of the budget was devoted to art. Unlike the obligatory work of art on the wall or the statue in the garden, *Open kamer* is a work of art in the public space, accessible to one and all.

Open kamer is a remarkable construction on the fringes of the care centre for people with a mental disability. The design defies the usual elements of architecture, at least as Rem Koolhaas describes them. You don't need the door at all to enter the open room, nor can you use it to shut anyone out. No walls separate the inside from the outside. You can step on and off the concrete slab easily. There is even a small ramp for people with a disability. Windows are not necessary to look outside. Nor does the room offer a roof over your head; on the contrary, it exposes you to the elements.

The work draws attention to a forgotten, primary element of architecture to create an interior space. Architecture begins with covering the earth, Bart Verschaffel wrote in relation to *Open kamer*, like a picnic blanket, a beach towel or even a table. In this sense, the concrete slab raises us off the ground, shuts out the dark forces and organizes a stage for human activity. The concrete slab thus defines an inner space, with the trees as walls and the vault of heaven as a ceiling. The status of the forest changes as soon as you enter the room. Suddenly the forest becomes your immediate environment.

The door is a striking element. The reflection of the forest in the reflecting surface makes the door blend in with the green surroundings, even though it appears the surface was insufficiently reflective. The door is of little use, but is equipped with all the fittings – hinges, lock, handle – and the heavy door leaf falls firmly into the frame. Its position on the far side of the concrete slab – when you approach the work from the central alley – seems to suggest that it is more like a passageway. The door is no longer an opening in the wall that provides access to the individual room, but rather a way through from the room to a parallel reality in the care centre.

This brings us to the somewhat eccentric location of the open room within the care campus, barely visible from the central alley. Armed with four sticks and a rope, the artist set off into the woods to find the most suitable location. Half a day later, he chose an unused piece of woodland at the end of the care campus, where the room occupies a place between trees and bushes. In this place, the work of art defines another place in the care centre, a place where the boundaries of realities shift. *Open kamer* thus creates a space of possibilities rather than fixed functions. Depending on the moment, the room is a place of refuge, a meeting place, a stage or even the setting for wedding photos.

The idiosyncratic programme of *Open kamer* thus points to perhaps the most difficult design challenge for the inclusion of people with an intellectual disability. All in all, designing residential facilities is an easy task compared to designing public space as a place of meeting and confrontation. Sockets lie hidden under the concrete slab for connecting sound, images or lights. At the same time, *Open kamer* is close to footpaths and thus creates an opportunity to attract passers-by. The work of art is thus an unexpected place where care is revealed and outsiders unexpectedly participate in the world of care.

PROJECT NAME
Zonnebloem
DESIGN
Architectuurgroep Jo Peeters
CLIENT
Monnikenheide vzw
LOCATION
Monnikendreef 3, 2980 Zoersel
DESIGN
2009
DELIVERY
2010
MAIN CONTRACTOR
Noordbouw nv
STUDY OFFICE STABILITY
D'Haeyer-Van Himbeeck & Partners nv
STUDY OFFICE TECHNOLOGIES
IRS Studiebureau bvba
SURFACE
334 m²
TOTAL BUILDING COST
377,386 euro
TOTAL BUILDING COST M²
1,129 euro
PHOTOGRAPHY
Dries Luyten

SMALL-SCALE LIVING WITH HIGH CARE REQUIREMENTS

On the border of the Monnikenheide estate, an elongated extension with wooden cladding and glass façades leans against an old brick house. Eight people with a severe mental and physical disability live in Zonnebloem (Sunflower). Zonnebloem is the renovation of Monnikenhuis, a building dating from 1985. The 2009 conversion by Architectuurgroep Jo Peeters reflects the history of a remarkable quest for independence among people with high care requirements. The house is also commonly known as the Orangerie, an allusion to the large veranda that was built onto the living room in the 1990s.

Zonnebloem is a hybrid volume, with on the one hand a red-brick house with a gable roof and on the other a wing with wooden cladding, large windows and flat roofs. The glass façade continues above the roof edge and is emphasized with an LED strip. The invisible window frame ensures that the wooded surroundings virtually extend into the interior. The wooden rafters and stone walls of the existing house were painted white. Acoustic panels on the ceiling ensure a peaceful atmosphere. The sense of openness in the house was heightened by moving the kitchen and creating a free passage from the new front door to the corridor.

The corridor runs from the living area in the original house to a seating area at the end of the corridor. The linoleum floor runs through the entire building and was partly erected as a buffer wall for wheelchair and care-bed traffic. The sitting area is furnished with a couch or so-called day bed and functions as a second living area. It is intended as a place of rest where residents can retreat without having to go to their bedrooms. The room at the end of the corridor was a first. Since then, it has been a standard feature of the programme of requirements. The risk of such an in-between space is that it becomes cluttered with equipment needed for the less mobile residents, such as hoists, wheelchairs and walking frames.

The renovation and expansion responded to the change in care needs. The original building was designed in 1980 by architect Luc Van den Broeck as a first initiative for independent living for four people. The Monnikenhuis (Monk's House) project was therefore deliberately located at some distance from the other facilities and given its own address on Schaapskooi (Sheepfold), the forest road that borders the estate. In 2002, however, the independent residents moved to Huis aan de Voorne (The House at the River Voorne), a 'project for sheltered accommodation' in the village. This increased the care requirements for the remaining residents on the estate. As a result, Monnikenhuis soon needed a lot of staff, which led to a doubling of the number of residents.

A characteristic of the renovation is the shift of the entrance to Monnikenhuis. In the original house, the front door was deliberately located on the side of Schaapskooi to emphasize the residents' independence. The opposite movement was adopted for the new situation: the front door opens onto a path that leads to the central part of the estate.

The house for residents with high care requirements, some of whom are bedridden, is physically disconnected from the main building. Staff support is therefore needed, especially for the night care. The practical problems are partly solved by sound sensors and cameras in the night hall.

The garden was designed by landscape architect Paul Deroose, who was appointed after Wivina Demeester met him when he served on the jury for the Bouwheer Prize in 2005. The design explicitly seeks to move away from the classic gardens around houses and rather create the basic conditions for integrating the care home into the landscape. Italian ryegrass was planted along the new forest path, so that in time the natural vegetation will return. The terrace was laid using the clinkers from the old terrace. A medium-sized hedge guarantees privacy while preserving a view of the trees. The garden attached to the individual rooms runs into the forest. In the garden stands *Drie Monniken* (Three Monks), a sculpture that artist Marc De Roover created together with the residents.

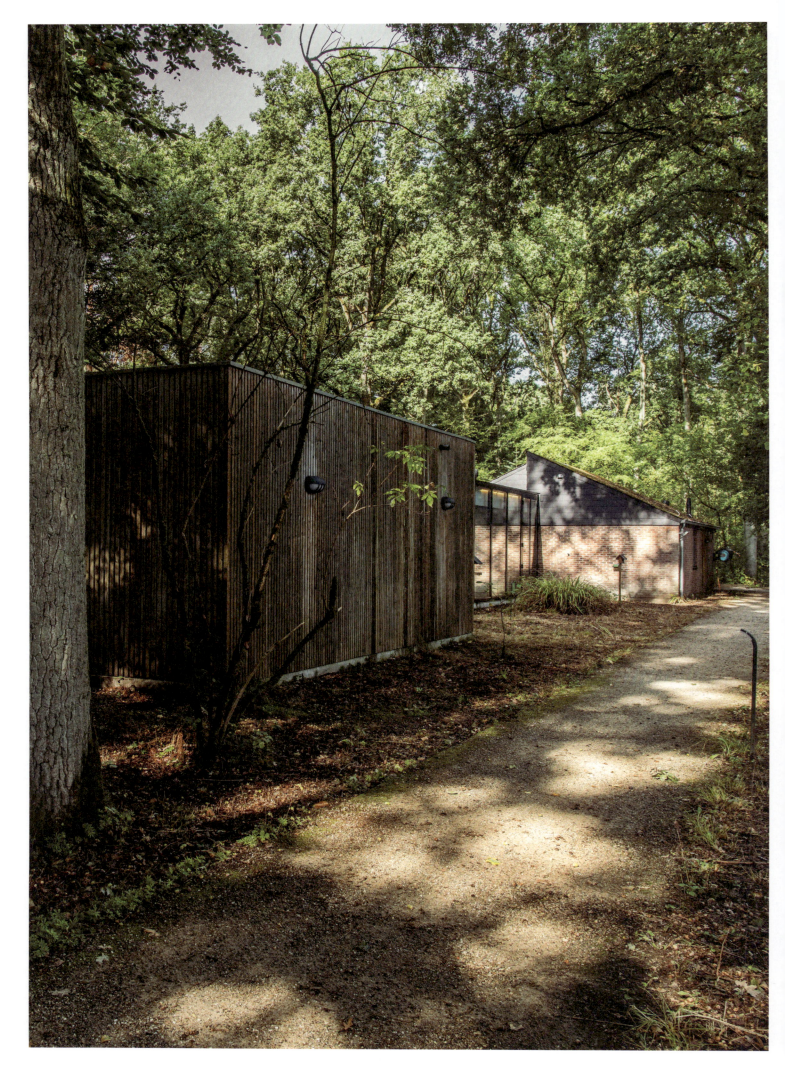

Level 0

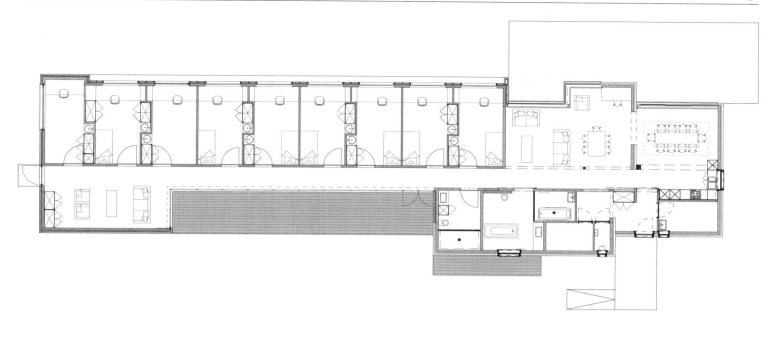

Section

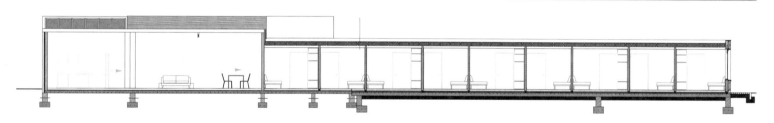

North Elevation

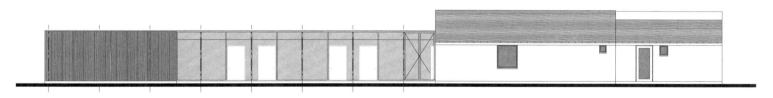

Zonnebloem — Architectuurgroep Jo Peeters

PROJECT NAME
Huis aan 't Laar
DESIGNER
51N4E
CLIENT
Monnikenheide vzw
LOCATION
Schaapskooi 16, 2980 Zoersel
DESIGN
September 2009
DELIVERY
September 2013
STUDY OFFICE STABILITY
All-engineering bvba
PILOT CONTRACTOR
Menbo Bouwbedrijf nv
SECOND CONTRACTOR
Group Zwijsen
SURFACE
1,320 m²
VOLUME
4,600 m³
TOTAL BUILDING COST
1,180,000 euro, excl. VAT
TOTAL BUILDING COST PER M²
894 euro, excl. VAT
PHOTOGRAPHY
Filip Dujardin

INDEPENDENT LIVING ON THE CARE CAMPUS

In a clearing between the trees on the edge of Monnikenheide stands a stately building with a blackened wooden façade. The façade folds itself around the slender trunks of the tall conifers, so that the volume looks different from different perspectives. Huis aan 't Laar (The House in the Clearing) was designed in 2009 by Peter Swinnen (founder of 51N4E and today active as CRIT. architects) as residential accommodation for two groups of eight disabled people who live relatively independently. The care home occupies a special position insofar as it translates the lessons from independent living into the context of the institute.

The key to the design is the vertical circulation space with zenithal lighting in the heart of the building. Two staircases start next to each other on the ground floor and rise in the form of a double helix. The rooms are arranged around the stairwell and in short corridors with a large window at the end. The two groups are not divided by floor but are alternated, with space on each floor for three rooms for each group. As a result, the staircase functions both as a boundary between the groups and as a meeting place, without any direct physical confrontation. 'The staircase plays on avoidance and meeting, presence and absence', says Peter Swinnen. The design thus forms the first springboard for social interaction.

The special staircase makes it possible for two groups to live together under one roof, while operating independently within the tradition of the care centre. Peter Swinnen responded to the request to build for two groups of eight people by designing a compact volume that seeks out the maximum building height in the forest. Besides being advantageous in constructional terms, the combination of two groups is also practical in terms of service provision. For example, each group has its own kitchen and living room, but thanks to the back-to-back positioning of these rooms, staff can easily offer support via the terrace. Even at nighttime or at weekends, only one caretaker is necessary to look after the two groups.

A second element is the whimsical shape of the building, resulting from the quirky design of the rooms. No two rooms are the same. In fact the architect calls them studios, not rooms. Each studio features a bend in the façade and has at least two windows. The bend ensures that each studio always offers two different views of the green surroundings and that the sun shines in at different times of the day. The location of the bathroom in the heart of the studio creates a U-shaped figure in which different atmospheres are possible for the access, sitting area, work area and sleeping area. This form also makes it easy to divide up the studio for the sake of privacy and identity. After all, the studio is not just a place to sleep, but also a place to rest, work at a desk or receive visitors.

Thinking in terms of 'studio' shows how Huis aan 't Laar incorporates the lessons from the housing in the village within the protected environment of Monnikenheide. Standardization of housing in a village environment is a good development, but it cannot apply to everyone. The residents of Huis aan 't Laar are relatively independent and are free to organize their daytime activities, but they require more structure. Not only their daytime activities, but also the spatial organization requires structure, says Wivina Demeester. Some residents cannot cope with the relative bustle of a village street and need a safe environment, but that does not make them any less fond of their own studio.

Lastly, the location shows the strategic stretch between assisted living and independent living. The position on an artificial hill gives the building a strong presence, even though the entrance is not directly accessible. The front door is accessible from the street in the subdivision. The winding path and private car park fit into the residential setting. Residents are encouraged to go their own way by the deliberate absence of a connecting road between Huis aan 't Laar and the central buildings on the estate. Nevertheless, the facilities on the campus remain accessible via a small detour along the forest road or the street. Because of the proximity, support from the care centre can also be provided easily.

Huis aan 't Laar forms a new link in the development of a genuine care chain that extends from sheltered housing in a care centre to independent living in the village. The main thing is to create various homely atmospheres in which different forms of living together can be developed, responding to the needs and desires of each resident. Respecting the individuality of people with a mental disability is after all one of the basic motives behind Monnikenheide, together with the belief that architecture can help achieve this objective. At the end of the day, the abilities of people with disabilities are not static and the demand for care changes significantly over time.

Level -1, Level 0
Level 1

0   5m

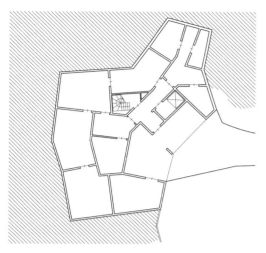
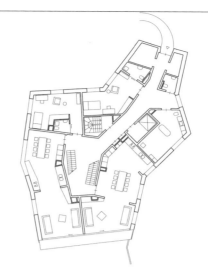

Section

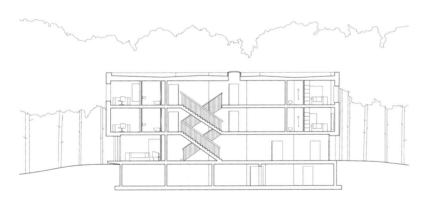

Situation Plan

0   15m

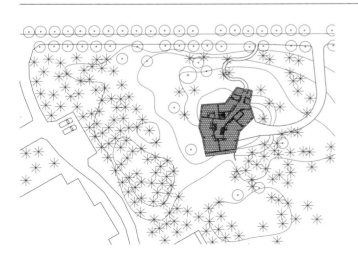

Huis aan 't Laar   117   51N4E   9

PROJECT NAME
De Eiken
DESIGNER
UR architects
CLIENT
Monnikenheide-Spectrum
LOCATION
Monnikendreef 3, 2980 Zoersel
DESIGN
June 2014
DELIVERY
October 2016
STUDY OFFICE STABILITY
Util Struktuurstudies
STUDY OFFICE TECHNOLOGIES
TECON groep
STUDY OFFICE TREE PRESERVATION
Bergen Boomverzorging
CONTRACTOR
Ageres nv
SURFACE
404 m², incl. terrace
VOLUME
1,344 m³
BUILDING COST
692,764 euro, excl. VAT and landscape
BUILDING COST PER M²
1,715 euro, excl. VAT and landscape
LANDSCAPING COST
25,805 euro, excl. VAT
PHOTOGRAPHY
Tim Van de Velde, except p. 120 and 121: Michiel De Cleene

LIVING AMONG THE OAK TREES

A new pavilion folds itself rhythmically around the trunks of an alley lined with centuries-old oak trees, at right angles to the central alley of Monnikenheide. The single-storey building provides accommodation for eight people with physical and mental disabilities and is appropriately named De Eiken (The Oak Trees). The building was designed by Nikolaas Vande Keere and Regis Verplaetse (UR architects) and opened in 2016. It replaces Rode Roos (Red Rose), an outdated prefabricated building from 1973, originally a staff building that was later converted into residential accommodation. Rode Roos was connected to the main building by a long corridor. Instead of demolishing the construction, an extension was added to the main building.

At the heart of De Eiken is the social area, which features a living room, dining room and kitchen. The position of the living room makes it possible to have a global view of all corners of the building, which is useful for staff and provides peace of mind for residents who have trouble moving around. At the same time, entering the building at the kitchen table has a normalizing effect. The kitchen table is the place for a first chat over a coffee. The design also makes use of domestic materials in alternating colours, such as orange curtains, a green floor, white-painted concrete block walls and a visible wooden ceiling. The floor-to-ceiling windows offer generous views of the large open garden at the entrance to Monnikenheide.

On either side of the living area are short corridors with four rooms and an adapted bathroom. Niches in the cupboard wall hide the room doors and ensure a transition between the collective and private parts of the house. Glass doors flood the corridor with light and give access to a covered and protected terrace. The rooms face the garden, so the windows can also function as an entrance. Receiving visitors therefore does not necessarily have to happen via the communal areas. This direct access from room to garden can also function as an individual terrace for residents who are unable to move around on their own.

De Eiken is an extension of the main building with an additional beam-shaped volume at the top of the long corridor. The reorientation of the rooms and the entry into the central living area is not the only difference with the existing communities in the main building. De Eiken is a key in the reorganization of access to Monnikenheide. The original assignment to renovate Rode Roos was cancelled and the new building was an opportunity to demolish the glass connecting corridor with the main building. This made the car park directly accessible via a footpath that runs along De Eiken to Seppenshuis on the central alley. This means that visitors no longer have to drive their cars onto the grounds.

The façade adjusts itself to a grid of trees measuring 8 m by 8 m, as a result of which they did not have to be felled. Nature conservation is not always obvious in a context of scarce resources, where investing in people necessarily takes precedence over trees. But the architects found an ally in Paul Demeester. The architecture had to make way for trees, rather than the other way round. A tree expert meticulously mapped the main roots and elaborated together with the architects a special design for the building's foundations. Today the building basically floats above the ground and the foundation penetrates like a comb between the oak trunks.

De Eiken thus forms the new face of the care centre. Ukrainian performance artist Anna Kosarewska created the work *Constellation* on the wooden cladding. It symbolizes the mutual relationships that develop between residents, carers, visitors and buildings. Over the years, Monnikenheide has organically grown into a set of relations. In light of recent developments, however, a second interpretation has emerged, involving the relation between the care institution and its surroundings, between the residents and the trees, and between the buildings and the landscape.

Level 0

0　5m

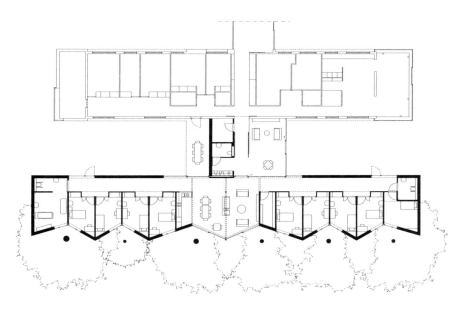

Section

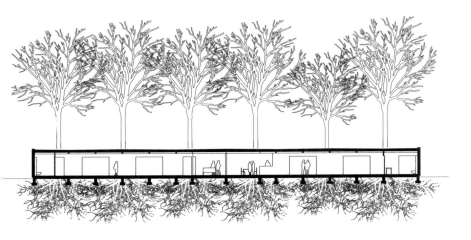

Situation plan

0　25m

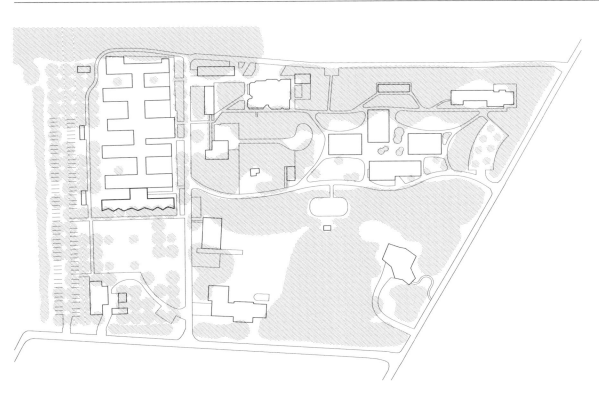

PROJECT NAME	Monnikenbos
DESIGNER	UR architects
CLIENT	Monnikenheide-Spectrum
LOCATION	Monnikendreef 3, 2980 Zoersel
DESIGN	June 2014
DELIVERY	March 2020
STUDY OFFICE STABILITY	Util Struktuurstudies
STUDY OFFICE TECHNOLOGIES	TECON groep
CONTRACTOR	Ageres nv
SURFACE	1,772 m² (prior to works: 1,168 m²)
VOLUME	5,588 m³ (prior to works: 4,480 m³)
BUILDING COST	2,618,246 euro, excl. VAT and landscape
BUILDING COST PER M²	1,478 euro, excl. VAT and landscape
LANDSCAPING COST	198,435 euro, excl. VAT
PHOTOGRAPHY	Michiel De Cleene

HOUSES AROUND A SQUARE

In a clearing in the forest of Zoersel, four virtually identical care homes are grouped around an open courtyard. The façades shine brightly in the sunlight. Chairs lie scattered across the yard, silent witnesses to a lively usage. Large terrace windows ensure an open relation with life in the care home. The design by Nikolaas Vande Keere and Regis Verplaetse (UR architects) meant a metamorphosis for Monnikenbos, a cluster of care homes built in 1980. It transformed an introverted and rather dark complex into an open settlement of three care homes and one therapy and day-care centre. Today, the new Monnikenbos is the new centre of gravity of Monnikenheide.

The care homes consist of three identical buildings, each with seven rooms around a common open space. The house has the atmosphere of a duplex house, with an open relation to a number of rooms under the sloping roof. The open kitchen was created by placing all the utilities (water, electricity, etc.) in wall units that could be shut. The various building materials remain visible and give colour to the space. Large terrace windows offer the residents a wide view of the events surrounding the houses. Dormers draw light deep into the house. If a resident wants to sleep under the roof but cannot climb the stairs independently, a simple stair lift is available.

The three care homes are arranged around a square with the therapy building/day-care centre in a similar typology but slightly larger. The therapy building contains communal facilities such as a TV room, a room devoted to Snoezelen sensory therapy, a play room, a time-out area, a physiotherapy room and a doctor's office. The front doors of the four buildings all open onto the courtyard, which has become a lively meeting place. Trees and lush plants grow in recesses in the concrete base of the yard. Low, artificial fences provide the houses with safe yet open front gardens.

Eye-catching pieces of brick and concrete-block wall betray a past history. After all, the new Monnikenbos was built on the foundations of the original building, designed by architect Luc Van den Broeck. After thirty years of use, the building was seriously dilapidated and suffered from many inconveniences, among others because care needs had changed over time. The fact that residents can live independently in the village centre also meant that the amount of care needed on the campus had increased. An adaptation of the infrastructure was required. In the search for a new future for Monnikenbos, started in 2010, it was finally decided to renovate rather than erect a new building.

A new demand for care all too often serves as an excuse for a *tabula rasa*. However, the architects prepared a design in which the existing infrastructure was preserved, although with a new façade and roof structure. At first sight, little remains of the existing buildings, but nothing could be further from the truth. The addition of a new shell made it possible both to insulate the dwellings and to drastically increase the habitable volume with an extra storey under the pitched roof and an extension to the individual rooms. New windows and skylights ensure a very light atmosphere in the house, despite its location deep in the woods. The heavy walls of the past suddenly appear as playful elements of brick and concrete block.

Perhaps the most radical intervention was the demolition of the central complex. In the old structure, the four dwellings were connected to a central space that was conceived as a covered square and served as a multipurpose room for group activities. The space was originally intended as a workspace but used for sports and games once the Werkhuis (Workshop) was built. This central space had no direct sunlight and offered no views onto the outside. At the same time, it served as the only front door from which the user could disappear into a maze of corridors full of nooks and crannies, entirely in keeping with the times. By removing this intermediate structure, space became available for a real square, which today provides a stage for new relations between the residents.

Ultimately, the new aesthetic symbolizes a new positioning of Monnikenbos within the care centre. The brick buildings with brown roofing slates used to blend into the green surroundings. Today, the light, striking façades with floor-to-ceiling windows stand out in the forest. The square forms the centre of the busy life in the various houses. The open work cluster establishes new links with other facilities on the campus, such as the animal pasture and the sports field, but also with other dwellings that used to function somewhat separately, such as Zonnebloem (Sunflower) at the back or Huis aan 't Laar (The House in the Clearing) on the edge of the estate.

Besides the practical advantages of adaptive reuse, there is also a strong emotional element at play in Monnikenheide. As Wivina Demeester says of the organized culture of demolition in the care sector: 'You wouldn't raze your own house after thirty years, would you?' The personal involvement translates into the design of care homes that make room for intimate memories and affectionate relations, not wards in the care institution that you can simply say goodbye to. The visible remains of the old brick walls symbolize this. Moreover, by phasing the work, the residents were able to continue living in their familiar places during the renovation and were closely involved in the renovation process.

Level 0, Level 1 0 5m

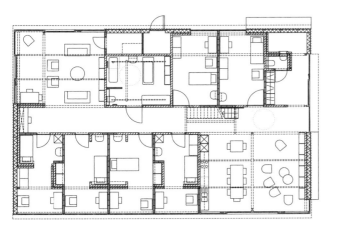
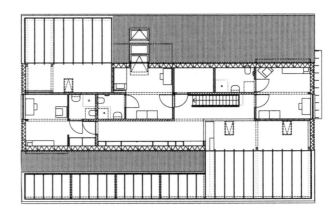

Section

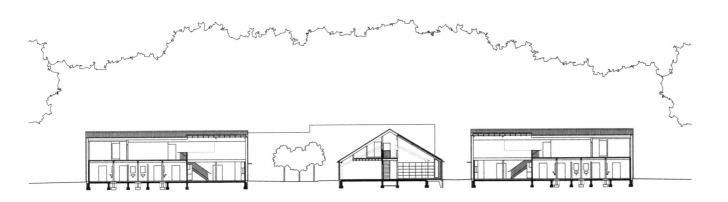

Situation Plan 0 5m

PROJECT NAME
Villa Kameleon
DESIGNER
FELT architecture & design
CLIENT
Chris De Roo and Emmaüs vzw
LOCATION
Langebaan 91, 2980 Zoersel
DESIGN
October 2017
DELIVERY
September 2021
STUDY OFFICE STABILITY
ROBUUST architectuur & onderzoek
MAIN CONTRACTOR
vanhout.pro nv
SURFACE
843 m²
VOLUME
2,768 m³
TOTAL BUILDING COST
1,357,000 euro, excl. VAT
TOTAL BUILDING COST PER M²
1,610 euro, excl. VAT
PHOTOGRAPHY
Stijn Bollaert

A HOUSE IN THE SUBDIVISION

A colourful, perfectly hexagonal house proudly takes its place amidst villas in the wooded subdivision. Villa Kameleon is just a stone's throw from the campus. The small-scale, inclusive housing project for eight people with a mental disability was developed in cooperation with the family of one of the residents. It was designed by Karel Verstraeten (FELT architecture & design), who was previously involved in the creation of Huis aan 't Laar as the project architect for 51N4E at the time. The geometric design conceals not only a radical transformation of traditional wards, but also an equally remarkable initiative in terms of commissioning.

The elementary part of the care home is what the architect calls the 'entity of the room'. A bend in the floor plan divides the room into a living area and a sleeping area with a bathroom. The floor plan of the room – in fact, a studio of about 30 m² – is repeated within the shape of the hexagon. The result is eight identical studios, each located at a corner of the geometric figure, thus providing unique views of the surrounding forest. Each room has two large windows plus two small ones, one of which lets light into the bathroom. The room is thus an opportunity, as the architect says, to do something 'radically different from the classic rest home or hotel room'.

The central hall forms the heart of the house and is also in the form of a hexagon. All doors lead to this hall. Eye-catching tiling gives unique accents to the doors. At the centre of the space is a sculptural staircase, which also serves as a light shaft. Strikingly there are no direct views from the hall onto the outside, not even through the doors to the living space. This makes it more of an introverted circulation space with no opportunity to linger – a place of brief encounters between the residents. The strategic advantage of this arrangement is that, when coming home, residents can go directly to their own rooms, without having to pass through the living area. This freedom of choice is remarkable in the context of care, where participation in collective life is usually required by the spatial organization.

Villa Kameleon is somewhat set back from the street, like all the other villas in the subdivision. The house stands in an open space among the trees, allowing sunlight to enter the living spaces. The footprint of the care home was limited and adapted to the existing trees, so that as few as possible had to be uprooted. The house is approached by a path along the side of the plot, where there is also a bicycle shed, an outdoor storage area and a car park. The entrance to the building lies under a small projection and passes through what the architect calls a small chicane: the place where you leave your shoes and hang your coat on the rack before proceeding to the central staircase hall.

Each side of the hexagon was given its own character by what the architect calls the 'facet-ing' of the house, the alternating cladding of the façades with cement and coloured tiles in three different shades of green. The reflection of the trees in the glazing makes the building blend into its surroundings. The tiles are reflected on the opposite façade where each window opening is accentuated with tiles in the corresponding colour. The tiles on the façades are repeated inside around the room doors to give them the status of a front door. The colours of the tiles contrast with the soft colour palette of the interior materials, such as the sand-coloured cast floor and the veneer wood.

A special element in the story of Villa Kameleon is the genealogy of the assignment. When Kirsten, a day-support resident, turned 18, her grandparents and mother decided to invest in her future. Summer camps, school trips and weekend outings showed that Kirsten enjoyed social contact. Therefore, the family started looking for a communal living facility. Inspired by the houses off-campus, they decided to create a small-scale, inclusive housing project for young residents in the immediate vicinity. After a free plot was purchased around the corner from Huis aan 't Laar, an offer was made to start up a project from Monnikenheide, including a management agreement.

Because the land was situated in a residential area, a subdivision permit was needed to build a care home with a mixed function. The initiators imposed strict conditions on themselves in terms of building height, footprint and parking. The intention was to limit nuisance for neighbouring villas as much as possible. Nevertheless, the arrangement of eight studios spread over two storeys represented an unusual change of scale in relation to the neighbouring villas with sloping roofs. After information meetings, the local residents approved the deviations from the norm, precisely because of the special character of the care project and the personal initiative.

Level 0, Level 1　　　　　　　　　　　　　　　　　　　　　0　　5m

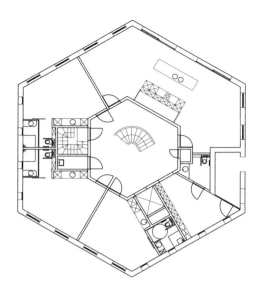
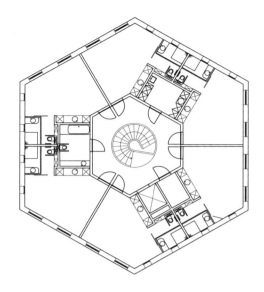

Section

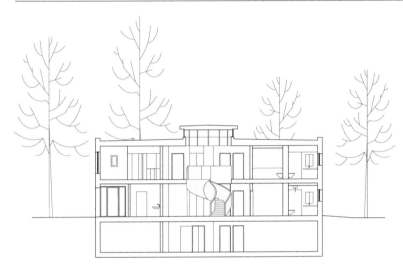

Situation Plan　　　　　　　　　　　　　　　　　　　　　　0　　15m

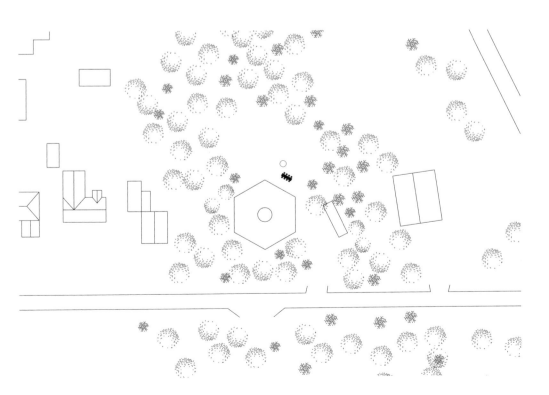

Villa Kameleon　　　　　　　　FELT architecture & design

ARCHITECTURE THAT MAKES PEOPLE MORE BEAUTIFUL
Sofie De Caigny

'From a distance, the shape in the forest comes across as more shadow than object. An apparition rather than a construction. The surrounding pine trees cast a pattern of fine linear shadows across the near-black surface in the background, while the pale green bushes form coincidental and transient layers of ornament. On closer inspection, the mysterious object turns out to be a building. [...] This, in the language of policymakers and professionals, is a care-sector building. Yet it is devoid of any hint of this categorization, and also free of the bureaucratically sanctioned references to 'institutionalized domesticity' or other supposed niceties. [...] this building is, in fact, an affront. It takes risks, as did its client – an organization that decided to build a house for people with special needs (and talents) in the woodlands north of Antwerp.'[1]

It is with this lyrical description of Huis aan 't Laar that Christoph Grafe, then director of the Flanders Architecture Institute, opened the editorial of the *Flanders Architectural Review* in 2014. The book brought together the most remarkable architectural realizations of the previous two years in Flanders and Brussels. The significance that Grafe attaches to Huis aan 't Laar runs like a thread through his editorial, in which architecture is envisaged as a joint project of the client and designer, deeply embedded in society. In this way, architecture can provide a high-quality framework for everyone, including people with special needs. At the end of the editorial, Grafe points out the crucial role of the Flemish Government Architect as the guardian of the architectural climate that makes these qualities possible in buildings.

What the editorial fails to mention is that several elements of the text come together in one and the same person. As the then managing director of Monnikenheide, Wivina Demeester was closely involved in Huis aan 't Laar, together with her husband Paul Demeester. As a minister in the Flemish Government, she established the position of Flemish Government Architect in 1998. At the time the *Architectural Review* was published, she was chairing the Flanders Architecture Institute. This essay outlines the significance of Monnikenheide for the development of the current architecture climate in Flanders and argues that this climate is difficult to grasp without the trajectory of its founder and first director, Wivina Demeester.

FROM ZERO TO HERO: CARE IN THE CULTURE OF ARCHITECTURE

The first *Yearbook Architecture Flanders* appeared in 1994. Subsequently, every two years an issue of the series would appear in which the state of affairs of architecture in Flanders was drawn up on the basis of the most remarkable architecture projects. The series, entitled *Flanders Architectural Review* since 2012, reads like a biography of architecture culture in Flanders. Initially, the *Reviews* rarely included projects for people with special needs. Huis aan de Voorne by architect Dirk Somers (then active with Huiswerk architecten) was the first care project to be published, in the 2004 edition. It was the first house at Monnikenheide not located on the estate in the woods.

1. Huis aan 't Laar – 51N4E © Filip Dujardin

The editors of the *Review* considered it exemplary for other care institutions because the housing quality received as much attention as the functional care needs. After the publication of Huis aan de Voorne in 2004, several editions passed before care architecture received renewed attention in the *Reviews*. In the 2010 edition, Gideon Boie argued in favour of architectural quality as an award criterion for care architecture. He argued that financial, technical and process-related parameters were not enough to achieve quality care projects. He set clinical functionality against the therapeutic value of architecture for patients and care providers.[2] In the same *Review*, André Loeckx discussed how architecture can mediate in the social integration of precarious people.[3]

Thanks to the texts by Boie and Loeckx, care and architecture did receive attention in the 2010 *Review*, although only three projects passed the editorial quality criteria for inclusion in the book. The year 2014 brought an end to this long period of silence during which architecture projects for healthcare appeared only exceptionally in the *Architectural Review*. Not only was the thread of the above editorial hung on the care building Huis aan 't Laar, but fifteen of the fifty published projects in the 2014 edition fell under care architecture in the broad sense of the word. Since then, the inclusion of care buildings in the series has become a matter of course.

The increased attention for care architecture also manifested itself in the broader architectural culture. In the 1990s and 2000s, cultural initiatives relating to care and architecture were few and far between.[4] In 2009 the Belgian architecture magazine *A+* devoted a special issue to 'care architecture', discussing a home for people with disabilities, a residential care centre and a crematorium.[5] A year later, Caroline Goossens wrote in *A+* about 'care and nursing'. She discussed the impact of the design, organization and scale of architecture on the well-being of the residents.[6] That same year, Maarten Van Den Driessche discussed the architectural quest undertaken for the Gielsbos care centre for people with mental disabilities. According to him, the essence lay in designing 'an "appropriate" rather than an "adapted" form of housing'.[7] In these successive articles in *A+*, the discourse on care architecture shifted slowly but surely from a utilitarian approach to a person-oriented vision. The architectural task of care was to place the resident at the centre and to strongly embed the care community in society. Cor Wagenaar confirmed this 'fundamental transformation within the care sector': no more closed islands, but spatial *and* social connections.[8]

Today, it goes without saying that good examples of care architecture are discussed in *A+* and the *Flanders Architectural Review*. This also applies to the broader architecture culture. Until the 2015 edition, care projects featured only rarely in the selection for the Belgian Architecture Prize; since then, care projects have been selected in every edition. Care projects from Flanders are also winning prizes abroad. The most striking example is probably the Caritas Psychiatric Centre in Melle by architecten de vylder vinck taillieu (advvt) and BAVO. The architects presented the project at the 16th Venice Architecture Biennale and won the prestigious Silver Lion.[9] The project shows how architecture is a story shared by clients and designers who dare to take

2. Huis aan de Voorne – Huiswerk architecten © Niels Donckers
3. Het Gielsbos, designed by Dierendonckblancke Architecten. © Filip Dujardin

risks to improve the living environment of many people, including, or perhaps especially, vulnerable people. The Flanders Architecture Institute published the catalogue of the exhibition *Unless Ever People – Caritas for Freespace* in Venice because the project's layers of meaning tied in seamlessly with the mission and values of the institute.[10] These are reviewed by its governing body (from 2004 to 2022, under the presidency of Wivina Demeester).

VANGUARD OF AN ARCHITECTURE POLICY

In parallel to the increased attention for care architecture in the *Reviews* and in the broader architecture culture, policy since the 1990s has also paid more and more attention to care architecture. Since the turn of the millennium, the Flemish Government Architect has occupied a central position in architecture policy. The Government Architect position was established in 1998 by Wivina Demeester, then Flemish Minister of Finance, Budget and Health Policy (1995–99). Convinced that the Flemish Government should be accessible and transparent, she strived for an architecture that embodied these values. She called this 'being recognizably present'.[11] Since then the Team Flemish Government Architect has assisted the government in achieving this by improving the quality of public buildings. For the appointment of the first Government Architect, an external headhunting agency nominated b0b Van Reeth. Demeester fully supported this choice.[12] Having commissioned him to design the Seppenshuis on the Monnikenheide site, she had already got to know him in 1994.

The task of the Flemish Government Architect is to support public commissioning authorities to achieve good architecture, to develop a vision and reflection on spatial quality over and beyond policy areas, and to act as a public figure with regard to architecture and public space. Throughout the mandates of the successive Government Architects, the set of instruments available for their mission has continued to grow. As the first Government Architect, b0b Van Reeth introduced the Open Call. Through this procedure, public commissioning authorities can appoint architects with guidance from the Team Flemish Government Architect. The Open Call was and remains very successful; local authorities in particular have been keen to use the formula. By the spring of 2022, more than 700 project calls had been issued, 319 of which have been realized. Of these, 7 per cent belong to the care and welfare sector.[13]

A second instrument that b0b Van Reeth called into being was the *Meesterproef*, which gave young designers the opportunity to win public commissions. It is through the 2000 *Meesterproef* that Wivina Demeester got to meet trainee architect Dirk Somers, to whom she entrusted the commission for Huis aan de Voorne. This amounted to a statement: to achieve a flourishing architectural climate, it is essential to give young, promising architects opportunities. To this day, this attention to young architects is one of the elements by which the architecture culture in Flanders and Brussels distinguishes itself from neighbouring countries. A second specific characteristic is the attention to the capacity building of clients, who have a major impact

4. *Unless Ever People – Caritas for Freespace*, contribution of architecten de vylder vinck taillieu and BAVO to the Biennale Architettura 2018 in Venice.
© Filip Dujardin

on architectural and spatial quality in Flanders. This is why Van Reeth created the Government Architect Prize, which does not reward designers, but rather outstanding commissioning authorities. To honour the founder of the Government Architect Prize, it was renamed the Wivina Demeester Prize for Excellent Commissioning in 2013.

From the start, the Team Flemish Government Architect has included an 'art unit' that offers support for the integration of art in public buildings. This attention to the significance of contemporary art in architecture and the public space stems from a regulatory measure from 1986 which stipulates that 1 per cent of the construction budget of subsidized projects must be spent on the integration of art. The measure remained a dead letter for a long time, until Wivina Demeester, as Flemish minister, dusted it off in the 1990s and actively began to promote contemporary art.[14] Although she never appointed designers to Monnikenheide through an Open Call – she did this through what she herself called 'a mini-Open Call' – she did apply the 1 per cent rule. For example, during the renovation of the main building, a small competition was organized that gave Richard Venlet the opportunity to realize the artwork *Open kamer* (Open Room) in 2006 at the edge of the woods.

Each Government Architect places his or her own emphasis and adds instruments to the work of the Team Flemish Government Architect. Peter Swinnen, for example, developed the pilot projects. Through the Care Pilot Projects, care architecture was given a central place on the architectural policy agenda in 2012. As the architect of Huis aan 't Laar at 51N4E, Swinnen had gained experience of care architecture that appears 'normal'. He baptized the programme 'Invisible Care'. In doing so, he referred to care that is 'no longer isolated from social and urban life but integrated into it. Care that is embedded in our daily existence achieves normality, self-evidence and invisibility'.[15] Together with Jo Vandeurzen, Flemish Minister of Welfare, Public Health and Family, a call was launched to commissioning authorities for innovative care projects. Five pilot projects were selected. Through design research and with the guidance of a quality advisory board, innovative concepts were developed, one of which was realized per project. In 2020 the Take Care! project expanded on the Invisible Care projects. The Team Flemish Government Architect, a number of architecture schools and several Flemish Government agencies joined forces to further activate the policy around Invisible Care with a five-part workshop series.[16]

Wivina Demeester was a member of the quality advisory board for the Care Pilot Projects as an external expert. She identified integration and normalization as *the* challenges of care.[17] She had been realizing these two principles with Monnikenheide since the late 1970s. With Huis aan de Voorne and Huis aan de Kerk in Zoersel, Monnikenheide showed how high-quality architecture for people with disabilities not only supports the lives of residents, but can also contribute to the visual quality of a village *and* to the social cohesion of a local community. Half a century later, the basic principles of Monnikenheide – integration and normalization – are still relevant in the pursuit of high-quality architecture for people with disabilities.

5. Award ceremony for the first Wivina Demeester Prize in the Atelier Bouwmeester, Brussels, 2014. © Tim Van de Velde and Team Flemish Government Architect Archives

THE PERSONAL IS POLITICAL

A long tradition of tension marks the relationship between self-care and public care, as Boris Groys recently demonstrated in his book *Philosophy of Care*.[18] Every now and then, there are figures who transcend this tension and make a contribution to the field of care in society. Wivina Demeester is one of them. Drawing on unconditional love for a child with special needs, she managed to move the architectural climate towards a living environment for society as a whole. She did this as a politician, as a client, as the president of the Flanders Architecture Institute and as a mother. In doing so, she embodied the feminist credo 'the personal is political' in a very direct way. All the roles she has taken on have influenced each other, just like the different scales on which she acts. In this way, a 'recognizably present' government has become an analogous task for architects and commissioning authorities, providing a dignified framework for every person, regardless of his or her limitations.[19] Architecture expresses both a view of humanity and of society.

Paul and Wivina Demeester's eagerness to learn and ability to take action are crucial to understanding how this vision was transformed into an actual improvement of care infrastructure and architectural policy. Their hunger to explore new horizons led them as the young commissioners of their family home to follow a course in architecture at the Lodewijk de Raet Foundation. They built a modernist house that spatially materializes the equality of each family member. This openness to architectural innovation also transpires in the choices they made for Monnikenheide. They did not opt for a house architect, nor for a fixed style or approach. Instead, each of the young architects they worked with was given the freedom to realize a new residential concept based on the needs of the residents. In this way, Monnikenheide became a testing ground for high-quality care architecture in Flanders.

According to Paul and Wivina Demeester, every building assignment requires its own research and an approach based on profound respect for the individuality of the users. This fits in with the philosophy of personalism, which was highly influential in Christian intellectual circles of the post-war Flemish Christian People's Party CVP (the present CD&V), to which the Demeester family as a whole belongs. Personalism strives for respect for every individual for the sake of their humanity, regardless of gender, race, status, language, nationality or intellectual and physical capabilities.[20] When, in 2012, Wivina Demeester explained why care architecture was an important social task, that personalism shone through in her discourse: 'Every person is unique and should be given the chance to develop their personality to the full.'[21] In interviews, she invariably repeated that the people for whom the

6. Policy brief *Vlaanderen herkenbaar aanwezig: huisvesting van de diensten van de Vlaamse Regering*, prepared by minister Wivina Demeester, Brussels, 1995.

7. Peter Swinnen presented the invisibility factors for care architecture in *Onzichtbare Zorg: Innoverende zorgarchitectuur*, Joeri De Bruyn and De Vleeschouwer, eds. (Brussels: Team Flemish Government Architect, 2014).

buildings are constructed should feel good *and* that architecture should be beautiful for each resident.[22] This vision became embedded at Emmaüs, the care umbrella body above Monnikenheide since 2015. In an interview about the special youth care centre De Leemwinning van Emmaüs in Mechelen, which was designed by her firm noAarchitecten, architect An Fonteyne said about the highly artistic staircase in the building: 'There were also people who thought the staircase was too beautiful for that target group. How can something be too beautiful for anyone?'[23]

8. Special youth care centre De Leemwinning in Mechelen, designed by noAarchitecten with art integration by Carine Weve. © Filip Dujardin

1. Christoph Grafe, 'Embedded Architecture', in *Architectural Review Flanders N°11: Embedded Architecture,* Christoph Grafe a.o., eds. (Antwerp: Flanders Architecture Institute, 2014), 9.
2. Gideon Boie, 'Plea for care architecture', in *The Specific and the Singular: Architecture in Flanders, 2008-2009 yearbook – 2010 edition*, Katrien Vandermaliere a.o., eds. (Antwerp: Flanders Architecture Institute, 2010), 249-265.
3. André Loeckx, 'The Architecture of the Awkward', in *The Specific and the Singular: Architecture in Flanders, 2008-2009 yearbook – 2010 edition*, 267–84.
4. Until the 2008 edition, the *Reviews* ended with an exhaustive overview of publications, competitions, exhibitions, lectures and conferences on architecture from the past two years. The list gives a first idea of the themes and players in architecture culture at the time. Only a small technical publication and a colloquium on psychiatry are mentioned in the overview, two projects that were not organized by architectural associations but by the care sector. See: Vereniging voor Technische Diensthoofden in de Verzorginstellingen (VTDV), *Integraal bouwen in de zorgsector* (Leuven: VTDV, 2005); Museum Dr. Guislain and U.P.C. Sint-Kamillus, colloquium: *'Heeft het huis van de psychiatrie een toekomst? Over architectuur en psychiatrie'*, by Dr John Van de Velde, Dr Marc Eneman and Stefan Van Sevecotte, with Joris Scheers and Noor Mens (25–26 September 2007).
5. Special issue 'Zorgbouw', *A+: Belgisch tijdschrift voor architectuur* 219 (August-September 2009).
6. Caroline Goossens, 'Zorg en verzorging. Open Oproep', *A+: Belgisch tijdschrift voor architectuur* 226 (October-November 2010), 68–71.
7. Maarten Van Den Driessche, 'Wanneer het wonen niets vanzelfsprekends meer heeft. Open Oproep', *A+: Belgisch tijdschrift voor architectuur* 244 (June-July 2010), 56–59.
8. Cor Wagenaar, 'Hoe gewoon is zorg?', *A+ Architecture in Belgium* 239 (December-January 2013), 68–71.
9. In addition, the project received a special mention at the European Prize for Urban Public Space in 2018 and was one of the five finalists for the EU Mies van der Rohe Award in 2019.
10. architecten de vylder vinck taillieu and Gideon Boie (BAVO), eds., *Unless Ever People* (Antwerp: Flanders Architecture Institute, 2018).
11. Wivina Demeester, *Beleidsbrief. Vlaanderen herkenbaar aanwezig. Huisvesting van de diensten van de Vlaamse regering* (Flemish Minister of Finance, Budget and Health Policy, November 1995).
12. For a detailed history, see: Jan De Zutter and Marc Santens, *Het Vlaams Bouwmeesterschap 1999-2005. Een zoektocht naar kwaliteit in de publieke ruimte* (Antwerp: Houtekiet, 2008).
13. Julie Van Holleberghe, 'Architecturale kwaliteitscultuur. De Vlaams Bouwmeester als maatstaf voor architectuurkwaliteit' (master's thesis, UAntwerpen, 2022), 19 and 103.
14. Stefan Devoldere, 'Dossier Kunstintegratie', *A+: Belgisch tijdschrift voor architectuur* 195 (August-September 2005): 34–48.
15. Peter Swinnen, 'Onzichtbare zorg', in *Pilootprojecten Onzichtbare Zorg: Innoverende Zorgarchitectuur,* Joeri De Bruyn en Stijn De Vleeschouwer, eds. (Brussels: Team Flemish Government Architect, 2014), 6.
16. Lisa De Visscher, 'Take Care!', *A+ Architecture in Belgium* 283 (April-May 2020), 15.
17. Wivina Demeester quoted in: De Bruyn and De Vleeschouwer, eds., *Pilootprojecten Onzichtbare Zorg*, 71.
18. Boris Groys, *Philosophy of Care* (London: Verso, 2022).
19. Wivina Demeester, *Beleidsbrief.*
20. Dries Deweer and Steven Van Hecke, eds., *De mens centraal. Essays over het personalisme vandaag en morgen* (Kalmthout: Pelckmans, 2017).
21. Wivina Demeester quoted in: De Bruyn and De Vleeschouwer, eds., *Pilootprojecten Onzichtbare Zorg,* 71.
22. 'Wivina Demeester en Erik Wieërs over het bouwmeesterschap en de Open Oproep', Flanders Architecture Institute, 26 November 2021, Youtube video, last accessed 12 January 2023, https://youtu.be/hIWesHtFYuQ and Wivina Demeester, 'Opinie', *A+ Architecture in Belgium* 283 (April-May 2020), 7.
23. 'De Architecte: An Fonteyne', Klara, last accessed 12 January 2023, https://klara.be/lees/de-architecte-an-fonteyne (accessed January 12, 2023).

Steven Demeester shakes hands with Queen Fabiola during an audience at the Royal Greenhouses of Laeken (5 May, 1981). © Monnikenheide Archives

VIVRE, C'EST FAIRE VIVRE
Thomas Vanderveken

In November 2020 I had the privilege of welcoming Wivina Demeester as my main guest on the television programme *Alleen Elvis blijft bestaan*, broadcast on the Belgian Dutch-language channel Canvas. In this show, we look at the world through the eyes of extraordinary people. Wivina had carefully chosen nine powerful film clips which she brought with her to the studio. During an hour and a half, I got to admire with her the creative minds and unique figures that had inspired her.

She couldn't leave out the musical *West Side Story*. It was one of the first records she got as a teenager. It's impossible to remain still when you hear those fingers snapping and feel the fire fuelling the story flare up. Nor could she overlook the perfectly timed humour of Toon Hermans. For her, his performances are still fresh: never rude, always humane and full of wisdom – classics. But I also discovered many new things during our conversation. For instance, Wivina introduced me to the extraordinary French designer and architect Charlotte Perriand through the documentary *Charlotte Perriand, Pioneer in the Art of Living*.

Perriand applied for a job with Le Corbusier in 1927 but was turned down: 'We don't embroider cushions here, miss.' She must have had a sweet taste in her mouth when, not much later, he offered her a work contract. Le Corbusier had seen some of her clever furniture designs at an exhibition and made a rather sharp U-turn. She would go on to work for him for ten years (on the very softest of embroidered cushions, I hope).

After her time with Le Corbusier, Perriand continued to put forward revolutionary concepts such as small flats and open kitchens with a bar – an intervention that literally and figuratively offered women more perspective since cooking and washing-up no longer had to be done in a state of visual and auditory isolation. Male architects, who usually focused on technical gadgets and neat interventions within a hermetically sealed kitchen, simply stood by and watched – before, one would hope, picking up a vegetable knife and chopping board for the first time in their lives.

'It's not about the building', says Perriand, 'it's about the person who lives inside it. It's not about the object, but the person who uses it.' Like Perriand, Wivina is a pioneer, a headstrong and progressive woman who found her way in a male bastion (and how!); someone who firmly believes in the transformative power of design and architecture. The right piece of furniture brings peace. A thoughtful design provides relief. An entire city, an entire country, benefits from a more conscious approach to what surrounds us. Space can serve people, help them live the way they want to live.

You'd be forgiven for thinking that the inspired woman opposite me – dressed in black, her bright eyes behind fine glasses – is an architect. In fact, she studied agronomy in Ghent and then ended up in politics. Wivina didn't sit on the side-lines: a minister for fourteen years, she also served as state secretary at a time when powerful women in Belgian politics could be counted on one hand. Behind every strong man is a strong woman, they say – the

1. Still from the film *Zie mij doen* (Watch Me Do) directed by Klara Van Es, 2018. © Cassette for timescapes

Demeesters turned that around. 'Paul was the best', Wivina says in the broadcast. With her unmatched self-confidence, she chose 'the best' agronomist of her year. And life proved her right.

In 1974 she was elected – to her own surprise – to the Belgian Chamber of Representatives and in the process became a member of the Flemish Culture Council, the forerunner of the Flemish Parliament. In 1982 she became a municipal councillor in Zoersel, a position she held for eighteen years. Barely three years later, she became Federal Secretary for Public Health and for Disability Policy. How wonderful, a woman with political ambitions! Unfortunately, not all her fellow party members were very eager to give her career a boost. When she ran for president of the Flemish Christian People's Party (CVP) in 1985, she came up against considerable resistance. Even in 1987, when that resistance had subsided somewhat, she failed to get the position. But never mind. 'Every crisis is an opportunity' is one of her mottos. Wivina became Federal State Secretary for Finance in 1988. She broke through a few glass ceilings afterwards as well, becoming Federal Minister for Budget in 1991. In the years that followed, she was Flemish Minister for Finance, Budget, Welfare and Health Policy. She concluded her political career as a Flemish MP.

For no less than thirty years, she devoted herself to her political responsibilities. She felt particularly concerned about issues related to health, emancipation and culture. And what really matters is that she changed those sectors for good. For instance, Wivina introduced a law on integration allowance for people with disabilities. This allowance is intended to compensate the additional costs incurred by participating in social life. Wivina was also behind the decree on voluntary work. She is a force of nature credited with establishing an HIV policy in Belgium, a smoking ban in public buildings and a decree on quality care in care facilities.

Where she finds the time is anyone's guess, but in addition to her political mandates, Wivina also took on several board mandates: University Hospital Antwerp, Flemish Cancer Society, Flanders Architecture Institute, Flemish-Dutch Huis deBuren, De Singel, Ray of Hope, Dexia, Lantis and Taskforce Westerschelde, among others. The list is truly impressive. And all of them can count on her insights and support.

And that evening in November 2020, she also made time to talk to me. She spoke with rare candour about the cards life had dealt her. About the times when, for a moment, the foundations seemed to tremble. The first film clips we watched together during *Alleen Elvis blijft bestaan* came from Klara Van Es's documentary *Zie mij doen* (Watch Me Do). The film was shot at Monnikenheide, an extraordinary place that is home to people with mental and physical disabilities. Working there as a volunteer, Van Es took the time to get to know the place and its residents thoroughly. The rich emotional life of Mathias and his neighbours was brought out in all its nuances. Poetry in black and white.

Monnikenheide basically tells me everything I need to know about who Wivina Demeester is. That it takes a village to raise a child is, for many parents, a hope, a complaint or a relief. Wivina Demeester not only *dreamed* of a

2. Still from the film *Zie mij doen* (Watch Me Do) directed by Klara Van Es, 2018. © Cassette for timescapes

village, but she had one built, by the very best in the business. She did this for her firstborn son, out of love for her family and other families in the same situation.

Steven was born with Down syndrome more than fifty years ago, at a time when society was still appallingly rigid in its response to such circumstances. I am not exaggerating when I say that she was a pioneer at the time, arguing that people with disabilities have just as much right to a carefully designed home where they can feel happy. Wivina knew immediately that architecture would be the key to that happiness. She opened things up – literally and figuratively – driven by the firm belief that a powerful and sensitive design nourishes and supports people daily.

The first years of Monnikenheide were hard. Wivina ran the place, cooked, cleaned the floors, placed tube feedings and read up on all kinds of disabilities in order to be able to adequately support as many people as possible. It paid off. Today, Monnikenheide is a wonderful home to more than a hundred people. Her son is also genuinely happy there.

Before Steven was born, Wivina and her husband Paul had building plans for their own home. Together, they attended a three-day course at the Lodewijk de Raet Foundation to get a better idea of the possibilities of contemporary architecture. A visit to Renaat Braem's house provided the right mental click: your home can (should?) be an expression of who you are. The walls, the windows, the rooms –everything can be adapted to how you live and function so that you can be yourself.

By chance, other attendants to that course were in exactly the same situation as Wivina and Paul: they too had a child with a disability. Talk soon led to the creation of a concrete organization, with its own board of directors. Thinking up large projects is something a lot of people can manage. Realizing them, however, is another matter. Often we don't feel competent enough, we get tangled up in the plans and often insufficient budgets, or our courage drains away as the months pass. None of that with Wivina. She was only 25 when she decided that Monnikenheide had to come into being. She defiantly rejected the customary solutions: there was no way that Steven and others in his situation would end up in an impersonal institution, hidden away, separated from the rest of society.

Wivina's father-in-law immediately stepped in: he still had a building plot, part of which he was happy to donate to the project. This site had once belonged to the monks ('monniken') of Hemiksem, hence the name. That was a great step forward, but more budget was needed. Back when crowdfunding did not yet exist by that name, Wivina and her friends raised two million Belgian francs by selling stickers at 20 Belgian francs apiece.

Monnikenheide was to become a warm place where people could live and be cared for in groups. Openness and togetherness were crucial, a sacred principle for Wivina. Over the years, famous names – bOb Van Reeth, Dirk Somers, Jo Peeters, Johan Decoster, 51N4E, FELT and UR architects – took care of the expansion and conversion of the pavilions in the services centre.

Wivina came into contact with some young and promising architects through their work for the *Meesterproef* of the Flemish Government

3. Still from the film *Zie mij doen* (Watch Me Do) directed by Klara Van Es, 2018. © Cassette for timescapes

Architect, yet another important part of Wivina Demeester's legacy. In 1998 she decided to shift Flemish architectural policy into a higher gear. Following the Dutch example, she established the position of Flemish Government Architect, bOb van Reeth being the first appointee. The goal was more attention and a more conscious choice for quality architecture in Flemish Government projects, together with the Flanders Architecture Institute. The result, in architectural terms, is that Flanders exists on the architectural map, not despite, but often thanks to several government buildings. The biennial Bouwheer Prize, a reward for inspiring commissionership in the realization of urbanistic, landscape and architectural projects in Flanders, was even renamed the Wivina Demeester Prize.

Wivina's love for architecture also could be felt on screen in *Alleen Elvis blijft bestaan*. Besides Charlotte Perriand and the documentary on Monnikenheide, she also chose a clip from the theatre adaptation of Ayn Rand's novel *The Fountainhead*, directed by Ivo van Hove (2014). The scene is set in a busy architect's office. We see Howard Roark – honest, idealistic and uncompromising – and his colleague Peter Keating, who chooses commercial success and social status. No prizes for guessing which character Wivina finds the most charming. Integrity – a word she may utter without any hesitation – is the supreme good, not only in politics, but also in creative projects. A good architect listens to the client and seeks honest solutions. This was achieved most brilliantly in Wivina's own home, which is close to Monnikenheide. The house – with an open kitchen, of course – was tailor-made for her and has continued to grow with her and her family through all the years and upheavals.

The Demeester house must be an almost magical place, where the energy bursts inwards through the windows. Because during so many years, Wivina combined her busy professional schedule with being a parent. I can imagine it very well and at the same time not at all. Today, of course, her children have grown up and flown the nest, some of them living abroad, far away. At this point in our conversation, we reached the moment that touched me the most.

People with Down syndrome are particularly vulnerable to dementia, often at a relatively young age. Steven is no exception. His hard-won achievements and independence are waning. 'What you spent a lifetime building up is systematically disappearing.' What many people experience with their elderly parents is something Wivina has seen happen to her child. And that is precisely why she explicitly expressed the desire to outlive her eldest son so that she can give him what he needs until his very last day. A bewildering insight into a mother's heart, but one that should not be misunderstood. Politics has not made that heart tough and cynical, quite the contrary.

'Vivre, c'est faire vivre', says Charlotte Perriand in the documentary, suggesting that to live is to let live and not just *'faire tourner la machine'*, which is merely about keeping things running. If anyone has ensured that others can live their lives to the full by waking up every day in a place that honours them and breathes life into them, it is this extraordinary woman.

4. Still from the film *Zie mij doen* (Watch Me Do) directed by Klara Van Es, 2018. © Cassette for timescapes

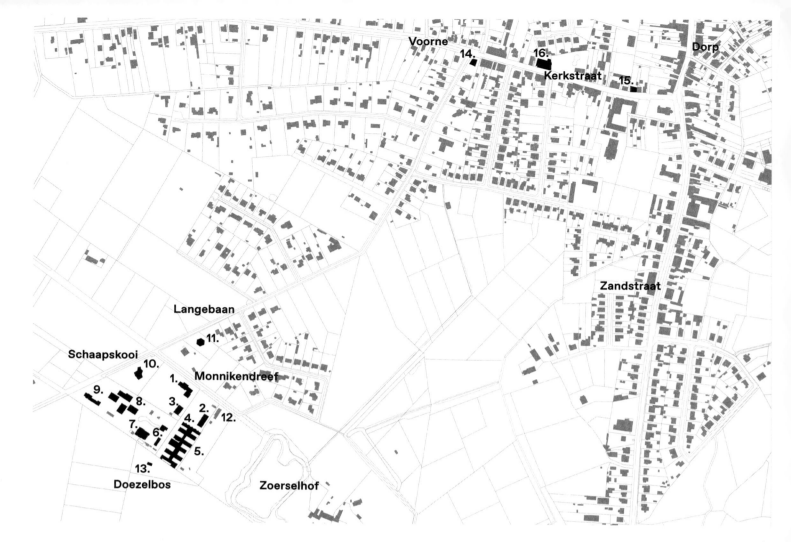

1. Demeester residence
2. Former staff building
3. Seppenshuis
4. De Eiken
5. Main building
6. Therapy Pool and Laundry
7. Werkhuis
8. Monnikenbos
9. Zonnebloem
10. Huis aan 't Laar
11. Villa Kameleon
12. Parking
13. Open kamer
14. Huis aan de Voorne
15. Huis aan de Kerk
16. Smoutmolen

AFTERWORD
ON AND OFF MONNIKENHEIDE

When you read the accounts and reflections below, you will come across something that we in the office of the Flemish Government Architect have always set great store by: the role of the client. The first Government Architect, bOb Van Reeth, argued from the beginning that it was not only the designer, but also the client, who must set high ambitions to achieve quality architecture. Since then, the Team Flemish Government Architect has always made sure to keep this approach on the agenda.

Today, this starting point is proving more valuable than ever. For public infrastructure in particular, the challenges for future-proof architecture lie not only in the answer, but also in the questions raised. It is best to set the bar high as early as the project definition stage. Guided by my team, as Government Architect I have become more and more convinced of the importance of the role of the client. In the past, I believed more in the genius of the designer and was convinced that selecting the right designer would lead to architectural quality. But designing is something you do in dialogue; you need someone to ask the right questions.

Wivina and Paul Demeester asked the right questions. They articulated the challenges in the field so accurately that any decent designer who listened to them carefully was well on the way to architectural quality. Not only were they exemplary commissioners, but Wivina Demeester also helped to establish the office of the Flemish Government Architect. She thus played an important role in promoting architectural quality in Flanders.

Good commissionership involves more than drawing up a list of requirements. It is about focusing on precise social values and ambitions. The clients of Monnikenheide chose a place on or outside the estate that corresponded to a therapeutic need. They positioned housing, work and care alongside or in relation to each other in such a way that they could respond to new social insights.

Thus, over the course of the assignments, they built or converted a residential and work environment for their family and a group of fellow residents in a wooded area. Like moving pieces on a chessboard, one by one they placed the functions where they belonged on the estate.

For example, they carefully chose the location of the first facilities for independent assisted living off the estate and closer to the village centre. This location invites residents not only to turn their attention to the estate, but also to explore the village. By buying the right plot on the boundary with the village and later even in the village centre, the commissioner defined an important social ambition even before the architects set to work.

The (often young) architects were offered the rare opportunity to translate this narrative into architecture. The quality of the architecture is therefore visible not only in the ingenious typologies that seek to combine house and institution, or in the materials and colours that so define contextual architecture in Flanders, but also in the social commitment that the buildings convey.

The buildings in Monnikenheide show how architectural quality can be developed: the commissioners determined the added social value by indicating the position and thereby the relation to the context, while the designer translated this ambition into special houses for special people who are part of the village or the woods – or rather, part of the community that connects the village and the woods.

Erik Wieërs
Flemish Government Architect

BIOGRAPHIES

Gideon Boie
Gideon Boie is an architect-philosopher, co-founder of the BAVO collective and visiting professor at the KU Leuven Faculty of Architecture. His research focuses on the political dimension of art, architecture and urban planning. BAVO expands the function of criticism by actively engaging with practice. Its research into the architecture of psychiatry received international recognition with the PC Caritas project – see *Unless Ever People* (2018) with architecten de vylder vinck taillieu.

Sofie De Caigny
Sofie De Caigny is director of the Flanders Architecture Institute and visiting professor in Architecture Critique at the University of Antwerp Faculty of Design Sciences. Her doctoral thesis focused on housing culture in Flanders between the world wars. She has published widely on recent architecture in Flanders and the relationship between heritage and contemporary architecture. She was commissioner of the Belgian entry for the 17th Venice Architecture Biennale.

Kurt Deruyter
Kurt Deruyter studied sociology and journalism, but soon found that the language of images offered him more opportunities than words to tell his stories. In a lyrical-philosophical style that is partly composed of writing but also questions our perceptions, he examines specific biotopes and how landscape and population dynamically influence each other. In the long-running project *Halfway Home*, he looks at the arrival neighbourhoods of Brussels; in *Caïn & Abel*, the native nomads of Siberia; and in *Rêveries du Promeneur Solitaire*, the mountain landscapes of the Pyrenees. His work can be found in museums and private collections.

Fredie Floré
Fredie Floré is professor in history of architecture and interiors at the KU Leuven Faculty of Architecture. She wrote a PhD on discourses on 'better living' in Belgium in the period 1945-1958 (2010). Currently her research focuses on the representational role of architecture and interiors in the 20th and 21st century. Floré is founding member of the research group Architecture Interiority Inhabitation. She co-edited *The Politics of Furniture. Identity, Diplomacy and Persuasion in Post-war Interiors* (2017) with Cammie McAtee and was guest editor of 'Architecture and Bureaucracy' in *Architectural History* (2022) with Ricardo Costa Agarez and Rika Devos.

Ine Meganck
Ine Meganck is a graphic designer, teacher and researcher. She has been teaching graphic design at the Royal Academy of Fine Arts in Antwerp since 2019, and from 2022 also at KASK School Of Arts Ghent. She graduated from Werkplaats Typografie in Arnhem in 2012.

Vjera Sleutel
Vjera Sleutel obtained a Master in Architecture from the KU Leuven Faculty of Architecture in 2017. Since then, she has gained research experience at BAVO, working on diverse projects relating to care architecture, especially within mental health care. She has worked in several architectural offices. She also developed her own art practice with Vroomm.collectif. Since 2021, she has been a Lab-O practice assistant at the KU Leuven Faculty of Architecture.

Thomas Vanderveken
Thomas Vanderveken studied music theory and piano at the Royal Conservatory in Brussels before starting a career as a presenter, first with the youth channel JIMtv, and next with the classical radio channel Klara. Since 2004, Thomas Vanderveken has been a radio and television producer at VRT. He achieved recognition with the talk-show *Alleen Elvis blijft bestaan* (Only Elvis Survives) on the Belgian Dutch-language television channel Canvas, where he conducts interviews with famous personalities.

Heleen Verheyden
Heleen Verheyden studied Art History at KU Leuven and Paris IV Sorbonne, and in 2017 she obtained a Master in Architecture at the KU Leuven Faculty of Architecture. Her work focuses on the social impact of architecture and urbanism and the search for spatial justice. It combines methods from spatial practice, such as mapping and research-by-design, with ethnographic research. She is currently preparing a PhD on housing for refugees at KU Leuven.

COLOPHON

Living in Monnikenheide: Care, Inclusion and Architecture

YEAR OF PUBLICATION
2023
EDITOR
Gideon Boie
AUTHORS
Gideon Boie, Sofie De Caigny, Fredie Floré, Vjera Sleutel, Thomas Vanderveken, Heleen Verheyden and Erik Wieërs
ART PHOTOGRAPHER
Kurt Deruyter
PROJECT PHOTOGRAPHERS
Stijn Bollaert, Karin Borghouts, Michiel De Cleene, Niels Donckers, Filip Dujardin, Reiner Lautwein, Dries Luyten, Tim Van de Velde and Wim Van Nueten
PICTURE EDITORS
Gideon Boie and Vjera Sleutel
COORDINATION
Barbara De Coninck
PRODUCTION
Petrus Kemme, Eva Pot
PRESS AND COMMUNICATION
Egon Verleye
DUTCH-LANGUAGE COPY EDITOR
Bart Biesbrouck
TRANSLATOR
Patrick Lennon
ENGLISH-LANGUAGE COPY EDITOR
Francisca Rojas del Canto
DESIGNERS
Ine Meganck and Isabel Motz
PRINTER
die Keure, Bruges
PAPER
Munken lynx 150 g
Maco Gloss HV wit 100 g
FORMAT
220 mm x 305 mm
REGISTERED PUBLISHER
Sofie De Caigny, Director Flanders Architecture Institute, Jan Van Rijswijcklaan 155, B-2018 Antwerp
www.vai.be
DISTRIBUTOR
Exhibitions International, Leuven
ISBN
9789492567314
LEGAL DEPOSIT NUMBER
D/2023/10.202/3
COVER IMAGE
Kurt Deruyter

This book is also available in Dutch:
Wonen in Monnikenheide: zorg, inclusie en architectuur
ISBN 9789492567307

Special thanks to:
Nick Axel, Jan Bruggemans (+), Beatriz Colomina, Johan De Coster, Ilse Degerickx, Kris De Koninck, Paul and Wivina Demeester- De Meyer, Sofie De Caigny, Gwenny Dhaese, Hülya Ertas, Nikolaus Hirsch, Erika Racquet, Jo Peeters, Dirk Somers, An Oost, Peter Swinnen, Murielle Vandermeulen, Klara Van Es, bOb Van Reeth, Richard Venlet, Regis Verplaetse and Karel Verstraeten

This publication is made possible with support of the Flemish Government

© 2023 Flanders Architecture Institute and the authors

All rights reserved. No part of this publication may be reproduced, stored in a computerised databank, or published or transmitted in any form or by any means, electronic or mechanical, including photography, recording or any other information storage or retrieval system, without prior permission in writing from the publisher. Each author is responsible for the content of their article.

The Flanders Architecture Institute receives financial support from the Flemish Community.